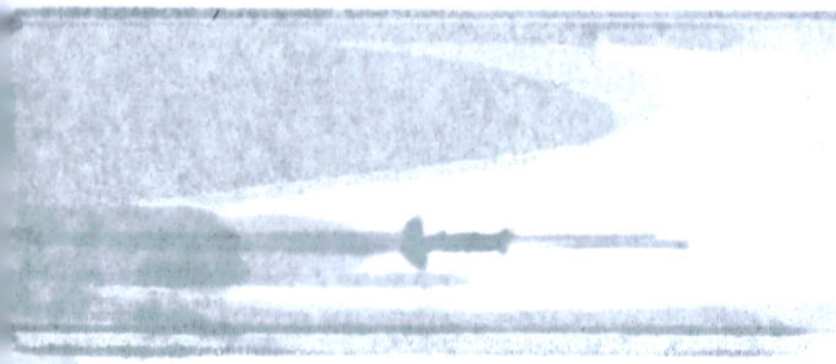

Artificial Intelligence and the Rule of Law

Artificial intelligence is an important driving force of the new round of technological revolution and industrial change. Artificial intelligence and blockchain have risen to the level of national policy. While the rapid development of AI brings convenience to people's lives, it also poses challenges to global changes and the development of human society, social governance and legal regulation, such as the leakage of personal privacy, frequent data security problems, and prejudice and discrimination caused by algorithms. AI is profoundly changing the world, and it is necessary to think about how to promote the construction of responsible AI from the perspective of global governance in the future.

In response to these issues, this series aims to explore and study the new situations and new issues at the intersection of AI, law and political science all over the world, to provide a legal basis for the development of AI-related frontier fields and to limit the development of AI within the framework of law to promote the harmonious and orderly construction of AI and legal systems. Based on the above purpose, this series is selected and integrated with multidisciplinary strengths to strengthen the research on legal, ethical, and social issues related to AI, focusing on laws, regulations, institutional systems, and ethics for the healthy development of AI. The authors of this series are all top authoritative experts and scholars in AI, law, political science, and other disciplines in China, and they have already made considerable achievements and social reputations in this field of research.

This series has a clear awareness of the problem and proposes specific solutions for the implementation and implementation of AI governance from a multidisciplinary and multidisciplinary perspective, covering AI, blockchain, algorithms, digital currency and other specific segments closely related to law, with cutting-edge, academic and theoretical value.

Le Cheng

Copyright Issues Related to Generative Artificial Intelligence (AI)

Springer

Le Cheng
Zhongnan University of Economics and Law
Wuhan, Hubei, China

ISSN 2731-6238 ISSN 2731-6246 (electronic)
Artificial Intelligence and the Rule of Law
ISBN 978-981-95-8780-3 ISBN 978-981-95-8781-0 (eBook)
https://doi.org/10.1007/978-981-95-8781-0

This Springer imprint is published by the registered company Springer Nature Singapore Pte Ltd.
The registered company address is: 152 Beach Road, #21-01/04 Gateway East, Singapore 189721, Singapore

Competing Interests The author has no competing interests to declare that are relevant to the content of this manuscript.

Contents

Chapter 1
Generative Artificial Intelligence and the Basic Framework of the Copyright System

In recent years, artificial intelligence (AI) technology has garnered tremendous attention and achieved remarkable development. As a pivotal technology spearheading a new round of scientific and technological revolution and industrial transformation, AI is profoundly reshaping the global economic structure, social relations, and governance systems. As an important branch of AI technology, generative artificial intelligence (Generative AI) has been widely applied in content creation and information dissemination processes such as text writing, image generation, and audiovisual content production. It has significantly lowered the threshold for content creation, while expanding the scale and accelerating the speed of work reproduction, adaptation, and dissemination.

With the rapid development and commercial application of Generative AI, the disputes and challenges it has triggered in the field of copyright have become increasingly prominent. How to strike a balance between technological innovation and copyright protection has emerged as an unavoidable core issue in the current copyright system.

1.1 Definition and Current Development Status of Generative Artificial Intelligence

Generative Artificial Intelligence (hereinafter referred to as "Generative AI") is an AI technology that leverages generative models to perform distributional learning on massive volumes of data, capture the statistical laws governing language, vision, audio, or structured knowledge, and automatically generate text, images, or other types of data with certain innovative features based on specific user prompts. Generative models are a category of models in the field of machine learning; they can learn patterns and structures from input training data and then generate new data

L. Cheng, *Copyright Issues Related to Generative Artificial Intelligence (AI)*, Artificial Intelligence and the Rule of Law,
https://doi.org/10.1007/978-981-95-8781-0_1

with similar attributes. Unlike traditional AI, whose primary functions are classification, recognition, and prediction, Generative AI takes content creation as its core capability and can produce new expressions based on existing information. In recent years, AI technology has undergone significant advancements driven by deep neural networks based on the Transformer architecture, and these improvements have fueled the prosperity of Generative AI systems.[1]

From the perspective of its development trajectory, the evolution of Generative AI has gone through three phases: early rule-based and statistical models, deep learning-driven neural network models, and current generative models represented by large-scale pre-training and multimodal systems. Early AI relied primarily on rule setting and symbolic reasoning, with highly limited generative capabilities, only being able to complete preset tasks in closed scenarios. With the rise of statistical learning methods, machines began to form probabilistic judgments through the induction and summary of large numbers of samples; although their generative capabilities improved, they remained largely confined to template-based and local simulation levels. After entering the deep learning phase, the use of multi-layer neural networks for data representation and learning has significantly enhanced AI's ability to characterize complex structures and abstract features, enabling it to handle complex nonlinear problems and exhibit a higher degree of realism and coherence in fields such as images and speech.[2]

In recent years, the rapid popularization of large-scale data training and general-purpose model architectures has enabled Generative AI to move from the laboratory to widespread application, with its role shifting from an auxiliary tool to a content generation subject. It can not only imitate existing expression styles but also continuously generate content with complete structure and coherent logic in highly open task scenarios. In practical applications, Generative AI has been widely used in fields such as text writing, image design, music composition, video production, code generation, and virtual interaction, and has gradually penetrated into commercial application areas including media communication, advertising and marketing, and cultural creativity, demonstrating unprecedented technological potential and industrial value.

The core of the evolution of Generative AI technology lies in the gradual shift of its content generation toward the learning and recombination of statistical laws and expression structures embedded in massive datasets, thereby forming a content production mechanism characterized by high complexity and incomplete predictability. While this technological development brings new opportunities for the integration of science, technology and industry with its robust application capabilities, its technical architecture has also begun to exert a substantial impact on the copyright system.

(1) Core Technical Architecture of Generative AI

[1] Xiaofeng and Xibin [1], p. 890.

[2] Hechuan and Yanhong [2], p. 106.

The impact exerted by Generative AI on the copyright system is not an accidental legal issue, but an inevitable outcome stemming from its technical operation. Whether it is the repeated learning of information such as texts and images during the model training process, or the ultimate generation of specific outputs triggered by user instructions, its operation always revolves around the imitation, recombination and extension of existing work forms. Generative AI has been closely linked to copyright issues from its inception; in fact, every technical link of it corresponds to potential copyright implications. A systematic review of the core technical architecture of Generative AI constitutes a necessary prerequisite for the subsequent discussion of copyright disputes arising in the stages of training, generation and usage.

By learning the expression structures and combination rules contained in massive existing content, Generative AI constructs probabilistic models, on the basis of which it automatically performs predictive generation and recombinant output of information. Therefore, the "generation" of Generative AI does not originate from free creation in the subjective sense, but rather constitutes an algorithmic recombination based on existing data.[3]

Unlike traditional AI forms centered on preset rules, current Generative AI technology in mainstream technical systems mainly relies on deep neural networks, especially Large Language Models (LLMs) based on the Transformer architecture, to conduct unified modeling of complex symbolic systems such as language, images and audio. During the training process, through repeated exposure to and fitting of large-scale datasets, the model gradually develops the ability to grasp semantic structures, contextual relationships and expression methods in an integrated manner. Repeated learning of a large number of existing texts enables the system to judge which expressions are more likely to appear in specific contexts, thus generating content that meets the user's needs after the user inputs specific instructions, which is presented in various forms such as papers or reports, audio, images, paintings, videos and software codes.[4]

The generative capability of Generative AI stems from the high-level abstraction and compression of existing works and data, which is built on the continuous absorption of the overall expression rules of human language, rather than the genuine understanding of the meaning of specific content. This characteristic fundamentally determines that its generated results are inevitably intrinsically related to the training data in terms of expression structure.

The technical foundation of Generative AI lies in the in-depth integration of two core technical principles. Centered on generating new content, Generative AI relies on the pre-training-fine-tuning logic of LLMs and the Transformer architecture to achieve efficient data processing, which constitutes the core of almost all high-performance generative models in the contemporary era. By introducing the self-attention mechanism, this combination enables the model, when processing information at any position, to simultaneously refer to the content at other positions

---

[3] Tong et al. [3], pp. 98–99.

[4] Yao and Shengli [4], pp. 49–58.

in the overall context and dynamically adjust the importance weights among different pieces of information. Compared with previous model structures that could only process information sequentially step by step, the model's ability to grasp the overall context is significantly enhanced, allowing it to establish stable associative relationships within a wide range of texts, complex image structures and even multimodal content. It is precisely under the support of this technical principle that generative models are able to accomplish diverse generation tasks.[5]

In terms of the training mechanism, Generative AI generally adopts the pre-training-fine-tuning paradigm. During the pre-training phase, the model typically undergoes long-term learning on extremely large-scale open data resources. By repeatedly performing basic tasks such as information completion, structure restoration, and content coherence, it gradually masters the fundamental rules of linguistic expression, commonsense knowledge about the real world, and the basic organizational patterns of visual and auditory information, thereby acquiring the ability to predict the next word in a text sequence. After this phase, the model internally forms a highly condensed representation of the distribution of real-world data, thus gaining preliminary content generation capabilities. However, a purely pre-trained model tends to only reproduce the most common patterns present in the training data, lacking the capacity to accurately respond to human intentions. To address this limitation, researchers further introduce a fine-tuning phase on the basis of pre-training. Through human demonstrations, instruction annotation, and preference feedback, the model undergoes additional training on datasets specific to particular tasks or domains. This process enables the model to gradually learn to generate responses in accordance with the specific task requirements set by humans, and develop relatively stable output tendencies. The volume of data used in this phase is far smaller than that of the pre-training corpus, yet due to the annotation and cleaning processes it undergoes, this data boasts high quality and clear goal orientation, which is sufficient to significantly reshape the model's generation distribution and evolve the model from a state of being capable of generating content to one of generating valuable content.

In terms of specific information processing methods, the Transformer architecture does not rely on linear word-by-word inference. Instead, it achieves holistic semantic comprehension by simultaneously correlating the relationships between different elements within an entire text segment. When processing long text content, the model synchronously attends to the relationships between the statements preceding and following key words, as well as the semantic flow, thereby grasping the contextual structure and expression patterns at an overall level. This capacity for centralized processing of global relationships enables the model to maintain strong coherence and consistency even when confronted with complex contexts, and also allows it to continuously generate structurally complete content over lengthy passages. The aforementioned operational mechanism is built on the long-term, large-scale absorption of existing linguistic expression methods. As such, while Generative

[5] Zubing [5], p. 149.

AI generates new content, it is inherently and inextricably linked to pre-existing human works.

From a broader perspective on generation mechanisms, contemporary Generative AI, beyond Large Language Models, also encompasses a variety of deep learning models designed for image, audio, and video generation. Despite the differences in their specific architectures, these technical approaches share a common core feature: they generate new content outputs by learning the formal structures and content distributions within existing data, and then recombining expression patterns on a statistical basis. Therefore, the generation process is essentially a form of simulation grounded in probabilistic laws, rather than original expression derived from semantic understanding. Inevitably, the generated results may be highly similar to pre-existing works in terms of formal structure, and in some individual cases, may even coincide with such works substantively. This consequently poses new challenges to institutional arrangements such as the rights of reproduction and adaptation.

Overall, pre-training endows the model with a foundational understanding of the distribution of real-world data; fine-tuning guides this understanding toward directions that better align with usage requirements; and the Transformer provides a computational framework for efficient holistic contextual modeling. Their organic integration collectively constitutes the fundamental technical basis of contemporary Generative AI in the fields of text, image, audio, video, and multimodal content generation. It also explains why this identical technical paradigm can be continuously applied across diverse scenarios.

(2) Key Technical Stages

The technical implementation of Generative AI is a sophisticated process involving collaborative optimization across multiple stages, with its crux rooted in the in-depth collection and meticulous preprocessing of massive, high-quality, and diversified datasets. The foundational steps in the training stage determine the breadth and depth of the model's learning. At the algorithmic level, built on deep neural network architectures such as the Transformer, the model undergoes intensive training through methods including self-supervised learning, backpropagation, and loss calculation, with its primary task being to learn the probabilistic distribution laws and complex structural patterns inherent in the data. Subsequently, based on user-input prompts, the model automatically generates corresponding content, and continuously incorporates new feedback during subsequent usage to adjust and optimize its output behavior.[6] It is within this iterative operational mechanism that Generative AI gradually evolves from a data processing tool into a content production system.

In its initial phase, the model is exposed to extensive datasets derived from diverse sources. Before entering the training pipeline, the relevant data typically undergoes preprocessing steps such as cleaning, denoising, deduplication, and bias correction. These steps ensure data quality, normative expression, and statistical

[6] Jingwei et al. [6], pp. 709–710.

distribution, thereby reducing noise interference and enhancing the stability of the training process. Upon entering the training phase, systematic learning of large-scale datasets ensues, encompassing various information carriers such as text, images, and audio. From a technical perspective, while this preliminary stage does not directly participate in content generation, it essentially determines the types of expression patterns the model can subsequently learn, thereby shaping the model's generative capabilities. When proceeding to the formal computation phase, the data is further segmented into minimal computational units, and converted into digital signals recognizable and processable by neural networks through technical means such as tokenization, encoding, and vectorization. Afterwards, relying on deep neural network structures and backpropagation algorithms, the model repeatedly fits these vectorized results, updating parameter weights by continuously correcting prediction errors. Upon completion of large-scale foundational training, large language models usually undergo a further fine-tuning phase. The model first undergoes pre-training in an unsupervised or weakly supervised manner, learning the basic statistical structures and expression logic of language from massive general corpora. On this basis, task-specific data is then introduced through fine-tuning, enabling the model to acquire more stable output capabilities for specific application scenarios.

Building on this, the model further leverages deep learning to gradually master the basic organizational principles underlying linguistic expression, image structure, and various information modalities. This process does not involve memorization of any specific work; instead, through repeated fitting of a large number of samples, it abstracts the structural laws and content distribution characteristics behind different forms of expression. After this stage, the model completes the transformation from a raw information collection to a general-purpose generative capability, acquiring the basic conditions for statistically combining and outputting content. Although the model at this stage possesses robust probabilistic prediction capabilities, it often lacks the ability to follow specific instructions precisely. Its output behavior remains largely governed by common expression patterns in the training data, and the generated outputs may be insufficiently controlled, making it not yet suitable for direct application in complex real-world scenarios.

In the feedback and iteration stage, the operational results of the model in real environments are continuously collected through usage behaviors, evaluations, and system records, and fed back into the training system as an important basis for a new round of model optimization. Generative AI generally adopts a continuous fine-tuning mechanism to perform reverse correction and optimization of model outputs, including instruction tuning and alignment tuning. Specifically, humans conduct quality assessments and preference rankings of model outputs, and then adjust model parameters retroactively through methods such as Reinforcement Learning from Human Feedback (RLHF), guiding the outputs to gradually converge toward aligning with human expectations.[7] To be specific, the model is not fixed after a

[7] Fengge and Haifang [7], pp. 125–126.

single round of training; instead, it continuously absorbs new data and evaluation information during practical application, thereby constantly adjusting its generative behavior. Developers conduct systematic evaluations of model outputs in terms of accuracy, relevance, safety, and acceptability by incorporating human assessments.

Upon completion of training, the model enters the practical application stage. The application effectiveness of Generative AI during the generation process is highly dependent on user prompts—i.e., the instructional texts input by users to the model—which serve to define the objectives, contexts, and expression styles of the generation tasks. By inputting specific prompt information, users effectively guide the model to infer and combine subsequent content based on its existing learning outcomes, make concrete selections among multiple potential output paths, and generate corresponding results in forms such as text, images, or other modalities. This process is not a direct reproduction of existing works, but rather a prediction based on probabilistic models. The phrasing, level of detail, and specificity of prompts significantly influence the model's grasp of content, style, and details during the generation stage. Users can dictate the final form of generated content by optimizing prompts and adjusting design parameters.[8] It is evident, therefore, that the outputs of Generative AI are conditional results shaped by the combined effects of prior training and user instructions, with prompts playing a crucial role in determining the final content within the technical pipeline. On the other hand, the model also continuously receives usage data and behavioral feedback from users during actual operation, and adjusts its generative tendencies accordingly. Through this continuous iterative process, the model gradually evolves from a technically capable generative tool into a relatively controllable intelligent system.

1.2 Technical Characteristics of Generative AI and Their Relevance to Copyright

Generative artificial intelligence is a dynamic content production system that is built on existing data, takes statistical modeling as its technical core, features predictive output, and continuously revises its own behaviors through ongoing feedback. Its operational process runs through three phases: data input into the training system, data recombination and processing within the model, and generation and output of content. Involving simultaneously the source of works, the formation of content, and the use of outcomes, Generative AI inevitably enters into profound relevance with the existing copyright system in terms of the legality of training data, the ownership of rights to generated content, and the liability of user subjects.

[8] Huiyuan [8], p. 17.

1.2.1 Technical Characteristics

Generative AI is a content production system that is highly dependent on existing data. The foundational capacity of a Generative AI model derives from the learning of massive training datasets, and its generation performance exhibits a strong positive correlation with data scale, data diversity, and data quality. Through cross-modal feature alignment and semantic mapping technologies, Generative AI gradually establishes a statistical cognition of real-world expression methods.[9]

The generative capacity of the model does not stem from independent comprehension, but is built on the continuous absorption and statistical processing of materials such as texts and images. The scale and quality of data determine the scope of knowledge that the model can cover, and directly affect the output level of the model: the broader the data scope, the more comprehensive the model's coverage of expression forms; the more unitary the data structure, the more likely the generated results are to be confined to a limited range of styles. This high degree of data dependence also endows Generative AI with the characteristic of dynamic updating in operation. A model does not enter a stable state after a single round of training; instead, it continuously revises its understanding of expression patterns by supplementing new data and iterating parameter weights repeatedly. Generative capacity is inseparable from data input. Essentially, Generative AI bears obvious data dependence, which in turn determines that its generative behaviors are always closely linked to the existing information environment. Given that the data necessarily contains a large number of works protected by copyright law, this further gives rise to issues concerning the legality of data usage.

Second, Generative artificial intelligence exhibits a prominent characteristic of uncertainty in generated results. Unlike traditional programs that output a single result under fixed rules, the output of a generative model is based on probability distribution. Rooted in the uncertainty of generation via probabilistic modeling, Generative AI does not rely on rule-based reasoning or deterministic logic; instead, it performs approximate fitting of data distribution through deep learning models, conducts probability sampling on this basis, and makes random selections among multiple probability distributions. Each act of generation constitutes a sampling of a vast array of potential results. The process of model output is, in essence, the stochastic recombination of these statistically correlated features.[10]

Even under identical input conditions, the results generated by the model may differ significantly, demonstrating a high degree of uncertainty and randomness. The uncertainty of generated content does not indicate disorder in system operation, but is an inevitable outcome of the operational mode of probabilistic models. Precisely because of the introduction of probabilistic judgment, generated results possess a high degree of diversity, and thus also exhibit the instability and openness that are comparable to human expressions.

---

[9] [9], p. 110.

[10] Zhen et al. [10], pp. 132–133.

Furthermore, the uncertainty of generated content will affect the predictability of generative behaviors. Users can impose constraints on the direction of generation through prompts, but cannot precisely control specific details of expression. Even when inputting the same instruction repeatedly, the generated content may still vary in wording, structure, style, and other aspects. The output content cannot fully conform to the definition of strictly reproducible content, and is closer to a probabilistically derived result generated on a one-off basis. The uncertainty of generation also means that the system does not have prior mastery of the generated content: the model does not comprehend the specific semantics carried by the generated content, nor does it perform value judgment or selection; instead, it completes content splicing in accordance with statistical rules. The output results do not possess directional inevitability, but only manifest as probabilistic "more likely" or "less likely" outcomes. Therefore, the content production of Generative AI is characterized by the coexistence of high efficiency and uncontrollability. On the one hand, it enables large-scale automated generation; on the other hand, it also renders generated results difficult to predict or reproduce.

The third important characteristic of Generative artificial intelligence is reflected in human-machine collaboration. The act of generation is neither completed unilaterally by the system, nor is it entirely equivalent to the direct creation of users. Human-machine collaboration runs through both the training phase and the usage phase of Generative AI. In the training phase, the model learns in accordance with objectives set by humans, laying the foundation for its generative capacity, but it does not possess the ability to independently set creative purposes. Both the data and algorithms required for training are provided by humans, and the generative capacity of the model originates from human choices of data, parameters, and training directions. In the usage phase, the act of generation is directly triggered by user instructions: users guide the generation objectives, content, style, and other elements through prompts, while the model completes the specific presentation on the basis of existing learning outcomes—the more specific the instructions, the more focused the generated results. The generation process usually involves multiple rounds of interaction: users can screen, revise, or reject the output results, and continuously adjust the content of prompts to make the generated content gradually align with the expected expression. The final output content is a product of the combined effects of human intentions and technical systems. This collaborative relationship determines that Generative AI is more akin to a highly automated creative tool, rather than an independent creative subject. Human-machine collaboration makes it impossible to simply define Generative AI as an independent technical system. Because the model does not actively set objectives, nor does it initiate generation tasks on its own initiative; the act of generation is predicated on the issuance of instructions by humans. This collaborative relationship makes Generative AI more comparable to a highly automated creative tool: the system is only responsible for completing content generation within the set direction, and humans play a leading and decisive role throughout the entire creative process.[11]

1.2.2 Points of Relevance to Copyright Law

Generative AI is highly dependent on the long-term absorption of existing data, and exhibits the characteristics of unstable outcomes and incompletely reproducible generation paths in the process of content formation; at the same time, its outputs are jointly accomplished by user intentions and system operations. Therefore, the copyright issues brought about by Generative AI are concentrated in three dimensions: the copyright ownership of training data, the legal attribute of generated content, and the division of rights among relevant subjects.

First, the issue of copyright ownership of training data is the starting point for the relevance between Generative AI and the copyright system. The model training of Generative AI relies on massive ready-made works, including typical protected objects such as texts, images, music, and codes. The original right status of these works is not unified, but rather fragmented, diverse, and hierarchically complex. Training data is derived from the continuous collection and reuse of existing works; thus, before the commencement of model training, the existence of rights to the relevant works, the identity of the right holders, and whether the works have entered the public domain constitute the prerequisites for subsequent discussions on its points of relevance to copyright law.

From the perspective of the object of rights, training data is not a holistic collection, but a superposition of numerous specific works. Each work already carries a predetermined copyright ownership relationship before being incorporated into the training corpus. Whether it is a publicly published article, a web image, a musical work, or program code, its copyright shall in principle belong to the original author or the subject that has legally obtained the rights. The training phase of Generative AI does not alter the copyright ownership status of these works; the inclusion of works into the model learning process does not mean that their copyright is transferred, extinguished, or absorbed into the model. On the contrary, model training is merely a technical mode of utilization carried out on the basis of existing copyrights, and the copyright of training data does not naturally decouple from the original right holders due to technical processing.

What makes the matter more complicated is that the sources of training data themselves are highly mixed. A large volume of data is sourced from the open cyberspace, which is often mistakenly deemed to be in a state of free use, but in reality, a considerable portion of such data still constitutes texts, images, music, and audio-visual works protected by law. The accessibility of a work does not equate to its free usability, yet this boundary has been continuously blurred under automated

[11] Wen [11], pp. 87–88.

crawling mechanisms. For other data sourced from commercial databases, material libraries, and professional literature resources, their use is inherently subject to explicit authorization constraints, and their application for model training will directly touch upon the boundaries of rights. Furthermore, the texts, images, and other content uploaded by users during the use of Generative AI will also be incorporated into the retraining system, further complicating and intertwining the copyright ownership, scope of authorization, and boundaries of use of training data. The training data of Generative AI is characterized by extensive sources, diverse types, complex development, and multiple subjects. Its legal attribute is manifested not only as an aggregated object of rights and interests involving different forms of rights and interests, but also as the concurrence of rights and interests among multiple right holders, who may raise new claims at different stages of data circulation.[12]

Second, among the points of relevance between Generative AI and copyright law, the discussion on whether generated content constitutes a work within the meaning of copyright law is equally crucial. In terms of its technical approach, Generative AI is different from previous forms of artificial intelligence centered on rule-based reasoning or feature recognition; its content generation capability is mainly built on large-scale deep neural networks, especially large language models and multimodal models with the Transformer architecture as the core. During the training phase, through repeated learning of massive volumes of data such as texts, images, and audio, the model gradually establishes a high-dimensional representation structure of statistical correlations between symbols, enabling it to perform predictive generation of subsequent content based on existing probability distributions when confronted with new input instructions. This generation mechanism does not rely on the understanding of the real world or the formation of subjective intentions, but rather completes expression output by virtue of complex numerical fitting relationships in the parameter space.

After the completion of training, Generative AI does not conduct content replication in accordance with fixed templates; instead, triggered by user input instructions, it combines, transforms, and reconstructs existing information through probability sampling. The texts, images, or audio output by the model often exhibit complete structure and stylistic features in form, and may also present a high degree of novelty. However, the generation process is essentially a statistically based "prediction of the most likely expression", and does not possess subjective consciousness or value judgment in the legal sense. Precisely based on this technical characteristic, the traditional copyright system, which regulates "creation by natural persons based on consciousness and purpose", has begun to face difficulties in application.

The originality required by the current copyright system needs to satisfy the minimum threshold of creative expression made by natural persons based on independent intellectual activities, and does not take the possession of high artistic value

[12] Taotao [12], p. 180.

or market value by the work as a prerequisite. The content output by Generative AI may formally meet the external requirements of "expression", but its generation is based on the statistical learning and probabilistic combination of large-scale existing data, and does not contain subjective creative intent in the legal sense. Therefore, it is difficult to directly presume that it meets the traditional standard of originality merely based on the external manifestation of the generated results. From the perspective of participation in the generation process, when the generation process mainly relies on automatic system operation and the user only inputs general instructions, human participation is more reflected as tool use, and the degree of control over specific expressions is relatively limited. The selection and modification of models, prompts, and parameters by humans in the process of AI content generation do not possess creativity within the meaning of copyright law, and the generated content is usually difficult to be evaluated as a work protected by copyright law.[13]

However, Generative AI does not always operate in a fully automated mode. Users can define the generation objectives, styles, and content scope through prompts, and continuously revise the output direction via multi-round interactions, thus endowing the model's generated results with the characteristics of human-machine collaboration to a certain extent. Technically, a prompt is a method of constraining the model's input space; its essential function is to influence the model's sampling path in the probability space, thereby indirectly shaping the expression form of the final generated results. When prompts are extremely simplistic and only input once, the generated content is mainly completed independently by the system, and the user's role is closer to that of a tool operator. Conversely, in scenarios where users repeatedly adjust prompt content and continuously screen and revise output results, humans' degree of control over the generated content is significantly enhanced, and the results are also more likely to exhibit personalized features. When humans directly trigger the creative act and contribute sufficient original expressions, the generated content meets the criteria of a work—a view that also represents the current mainstream position.[14]

Finally, in the application scenarios of Generative AI, the relationship between users and AI service providers is neither equivalent to the author-communicator relationship under traditional copyright law, nor similar to existing platform content production models. This constitutes the most practical issue among the points of relevance between Generative AI and copyright law. Content creation is not accomplished by a single subject; instead, users issue specific instructions, and platforms complete the output by virtue of algorithm models and computing power systems, forming a stable division of labor between the two parties. Users define the theme, style, and purpose of content through prompts, while platforms determine the content generation method and expression form by pre-setting model structures, parameter configurations, and reasoning paths. This human-machine collaborative

[13] Linghan et al. [13], p. 159.

[14] Ge et al. [14], p. 5.

generation method makes the formation of the final content dependent on both user intentions and platform technical capabilities, and thus its right division differs from that of traditional creative forms.

In terms of the technical process, users input prompts to influence the theme, style, function, and purpose of the generated content. What users hold is a right of definition, whose function is to determine the ultimate objective of the generated content. Platforms, through models, parameters, training, and output rules, substantially determine how the generated content is formed and the form in which it is ultimately presented. What platforms hold is the implementation method and conditions of generative capabilities. The formation process of generated content is different from natural person creation in the traditional sense, and it is also difficult to be simply categorized into the existing types of automated tool outputs. Compared with existing types such as commissioned creation, this generation process is characterized by the fact that platforms do not complete content output item by item in accordance with users' specific instructions, but rather provide holistic feedback on prompt information through abstract models. Users cannot directly control the expression form and sequence, but can only continuously adjust prompts to influence the output results. Platforms also do not make individual judgments on specific generated content, but rely on unified model rules for batch operation. Precisely for this reason, generated content is neither completely dominated by users nor fully subject to the free disposal of platforms; instead, it forms a result form with uncertainty under the joint action of both parties.

From the perspective of existing systems, current laws have not yet established special rules for the attribution of rights to such human-machine collaborative generated content. In practice, the right to use generated content is mainly divided through user agreements. Most AI service providers adopt relatively consistent arrangements in their user agreement clauses: users are entitled to the right to use and reuse the generated content, while platforms retain complete control over models, algorithms, data structures, and system operations. This arrangement functionally satisfies users' practical expectation of being able to control and use the generated results, while also ensuring platforms' mastery of their core technologies. Therefore, the issue of right division for generated content does not revolve around the attribution of copyright in the work, but is more reflected in a system arrangement centered on usage rights. Platforms usually do not directly claim to have complete dominant status over the generated content itself in the sense of copyright, but rather reserve relatively relaxed usage space for users through contracts, limiting their own rights to technical aspects such as models, parameters, and system rules. This also constitutes the most representative right division method in current Generative AI content production. To a large extent, this right division method still relies on the unilateral rule-setting of platforms. Since generated content cannot exist independently of existing technical systems, AI service providers actually continuously influence the use and dissemination methods of generated content through the design of interface openness, output restrictions, call frequency, and content structure. Especially in specific functional scenarios such as template-based generation, platforms' intervention in generation rules has established a closer connection between them and generated content, which is different from that of traditional neutral technical tools.[15] The complexity of the right attribute of generated content determines the inevitable adaptation pressure faced by the traditional copyright system when confronted with Generative AI.

Overall, the copyright relevance of Generative AI is not a matter of applying a single legal clause, but is closely related to its technical characteristics. Neither the copyright ownership of training data, the "work attribute" of generated content, nor the right division between users and AI service providers can be further discussed without considering the technical background. While generative technology has significantly improved the efficiency of content production, it has also continuously intensified its impact on the traditional copyright system. Relying solely on existing copyright norms for ex post facto adjustments has become difficult to fully address the legal challenges brought by generative technology. Only through the coordinated advancement of technical constraints and legal systems can a relative balance be achieved between promoting technological innovation and maintaining the copyright order.

1.3 Core Elements and Protection Logic of the Copyright System

The core of the copyright system lies in legally affirming creators' exclusive control over their intellectual achievements, aiming to balance the interests between individuals and the public. Copyright law takes works as its object of protection—namely, intellectual creations in the literary, artistic, and scientific domains that satisfy the requirements of originality and reproducibility. It designates authors as the subjects of rights, referring to natural persons, legal persons, or other organizations that hold original or successive rights to works. Centered on the content of rights, it encompasses both economic rights of use over works (e.g., the rights of reproduction, distribution, and information network communication) and moral rights safeguarding creators' spiritual interests (e.g., the rights of authorship and integrity of the work). The current copyright system has established a comprehensive protection framework covering the creation, dissemination, and utilization of works.

[15] Ping [15], p. 27.

1.3.1 Core Legislative Purposes and Values of the Copyright System

As an indispensable component of the modern legal system, the copyright system serves dual legislative purposes: not only protecting the legitimate interests of individual creators, but also promoting the prosperity of social culture and science, and balancing the relationship between private and public interests. By recognizing and safeguarding authors' rights to their intellectual achievements, it incentivizes the continuous creation and dissemination of literary, artistic, and scientific works, constructs a legal framework balancing individual and public interests, advances the coordinated development of social spiritual and material civilization, and thereby fosters the progress and prosperity of cultural and scientific undertakings of society as a whole. Below, starting from key concepts such as the definition of works, subjects of rights, and content of rights, we further clarify the legislative purposes and values of the copyright system.

(1) Definition and Protection of Works

The primary legislative purpose of the copyright system is reflected in the recognition and protection of intellectual achievements, which are expressed in certain forms to become transmissible and reproducible works. A work is not a mere creation, but a concrete manifestation of intellectual labor. Under existing legal provisions, a work generally needs to satisfy two basic characteristics: originality and fixation. Originality means the work is independently completed by the creator and possesses a certain degree of creativity. Fixation requires the work to be recorded or expressed in a certain form, fixed on a tangible medium, and capable of being reproduced and perceived by humans. China imposes a relatively lower threshold for work protection: reproducibility suffices, and even oral works are eligible; the United States, by contrast, requires works to be in a fixed form to be protected. The legal definition of a "work" under copyright law is of critical importance, as it directly determines which creative achievements can be included in the scope of copyright protection—work recognition is the starting point of copyright protection.

Unlike the property right system, which protects tangible assets, the copyright system regulates intangible achievements embodied in the expression of ideas. Once a work is created and fixed in a certain medium, it is eligible for legal protection. Without a sound system for right confirmation and protection, works are vulnerable to unauthorized reproduction and appropriation during dissemination, and creators will find it difficult to sustain investment of time and resources in creation. By restricting unauthorized exploitation, the copyright system ensures creators' control over their achievements. This not only provides incentives for creators to create and disseminate works, but also cultivates a sustainable environment for innovation in society.[16]

[16] Xiang [16], pp. 151–152.

(2) Subjects of Rights

The core of the copyright system lies in affirming creators' exclusive rights to their works. It endows creators with proprietary rights over their intellectual achievements—i.e., exclusive rights of use—covering not only basic rights such as the right to publish and the right of authorship, but also rights to distribute, disseminate, and adapt the works. Copyright holders generally include authors and other natural persons, legal persons, or unincorporated organizations that enjoy copyright.

When determining creators' rights, copyright law typically identifies creators as the original authors of works, i.e., the initial embodiment of creation. Therefore, creators are entitled not only to economic interests in their works but also to moral rights, such as the right of authorship and the right to protect the integrity of the work. The core value of the copyright system lies precisely in incentivizing creators to continue investing in creation and sharing their achievements through the protection of these rights. However, with changes in creative forms, the definition of subjects of rights has gradually become more complex. The emergence of Generative AI has increased the degree of technical participation in creation, raising legal issues regarding which subject the copyright of works should belong to. Nevertheless, the basic principle of the copyright system still emphasizes that human creation and the manifestation of human will should be the fundamental basis for determining work ownership.

(3) Content of Rights

The content of rights involved in the copyright system includes economic rights and moral rights. Economic rights grant creators control over the reproduction, distribution, performance, adaptation, and public dissemination of their works, ensuring that creators can obtain economic returns through the market-oriented exploitation of their works. Moral rights, on the other hand, emphasize creators' non-economic control over their works—such as the right of authorship and the right to protect the integrity of the work—ensuring that creators can safeguard their works and reputation. One of the basic values of the copyright system is to endow creators with this series of exclusive rights to protect the motivation for creation and innovation. At the same time, the copyright system also recognizes the importance of balancing copyright protection with public interests. To avoid excessive enclosure of public culture and knowledge by copyright protection, the system adopts the principle of "fair use", allowing non-commercial use under certain conditions. For example, in fields such as learning and research, news reporting, and education, the limited use of others' published works is permitted without infringing on the creators' basic rights. The existence of the fair use system not only protects the rights and interests of creators but also aims to promote the dissemination and sharing of knowledge.[17]

In addition, the term of copyright protection stipulated by the copyright system also reflects the balance between creation and dissemination. Works enjoy

[17] Qi [17], p. 236.

protection for a certain period after their creation; upon expiration, they enter the public domain and can be freely used by anyone. This design, on the one hand, safeguards the long-term economic interests of creators, and on the other hand, ensures that society can extensively use existing knowledge resources within an appropriate timeframe.

(4) Social Functions of the Copyright System

The copyright system is not only a tool for protecting creators but also undertakes the role of regulating the order of the cultural market. In a market economy, by clarifying the ownership of rights to works, methods of use, and licensing rules, the copyright system regulates the circulation and transaction of cultural products, maximizing the efficiency of production and utilization.[18]

In traditional industries such as book publishing, film production, and music, the copyright system helps creators reach agreements with publishers, film studios, distributors, and other parties. Through copyright authorization and transfer, it ensures that creators' interests are protected while their works enter the market and achieve commercial returns. With the popularization of the Internet, the speed and scale of information dissemination have expanded unprecedentedly, and the copyright system still plays an important role in emerging information network platforms, streaming media services, and other digital economy sectors.

Within the institutional framework of the aforementioned legislative purposes and core values, with the rapid development of artificial intelligence technology—especially the introduction of Generative AI into the field of content production—the copyright system has gradually taken on new dimensions. Technological progress has significantly improved the efficiency of work dissemination and enhanced the public's ability to access information and participate in cultural production. The system needs to reserve sufficient space for fair use and innovative use to simultaneously respond to the adjustment needs brought by creative incentives, public cultural supply, and technological changes. How to address the challenges posed by new technologies without deviating from the fundamental values of the copyright system has become an era-defining issue that must be seriously addressed in both theory and practice in the field of copyright.

1.3.2 Differences and Common Grounds Among Major Global Copyright Systems

Generative AI is transforming the modes of content production while continuously challenging the established copyright system. Copyright frameworks across the world are not identical, and countries have adopted divergent approaches in addressing the advent of this new technology. The United States places greater emphasis on

[18] Kaixin [18], p. 85.

market efficiency and freedom of use, the European Union prioritizes regulatory stability and the protection of authors' rights, Japan has clearly tilted toward technological utilization amid its recent legislative reforms, and China seeks to balance protection and development under its codified legal system. These institutional disparities expose Generative AI to varying compliance requirements across its training, generation, and application phases. Nevertheless, nations maintain a highly consistent fundamental stance on core issues such as the originality of works, the dual nature of copyright, rights limitations, and the balance between private rights and public interests.

(1) Differences

From a comparative law perspective, contemporary global copyright systems have not converged into a unified normative model. Driven by distinct historical traditions and legal frameworks, different jurisdictions have developed copyright protection regimes with unique features. Notably, the common law system represented by the United States, the civil law coordination system led by the European Union, and the codified law-dominated model exemplified by China exhibit marked divergences in rights stipulations and judicial discretion.

The copyright system of the Anglo-American legal family is grounded in utilitarianism, emphasizing copyright's role in economic incentivization and market efficiency. U.S. copyright law treats copyright as a freely transferable property right, prioritizing the protection of works' economic exploitation value, whereas the safeguards for authors' moral rights are relatively limited. The United States does not fully recognize the rights of authorship and integrity enshrined in the Berne Convention for the Protection of Literary and Artistic Works, unless explicitly stipulated in contractual agreements. The operation of the U.S. copyright system centers on case law, emphasizing judicial flexibility in adjudicating individual cases, with the fair use doctrine as its most representative component. Courts apply a four-factor test to comprehensively determine whether a specific use constitutes infringement. The test evaluates (1) the purpose and character of the use, (2) the nature of the copyrighted work, (3) the amount and substantiality of the portion used in relation to the copyrighted work as a whole, and (4) the effect of the use upon the potential market for or value of the copyrighted work, rendering case-specific judgments on infringement. This approach embodies a distinct pragmatist orientation: it does not predefine closed scenarios for application, but rather entrusts courts with balancing copyright protection and innovation incentives through highly open judicial discretion. Such an institutional arrangement demonstrates strong adaptability in the context of emerging technologies, enabling judicial authorities to dynamically adjust the boundaries of fair use in response to technological advancements and fostering flexible development space for new technologies and business models within the existing regulatory framework. However, it also gives rise to issues of high regulatory uncertainty and weak predictability for market participants.

Unlike the United States, the EU copyright system is deeply influenced by the civil law tradition, with a stronger focus on regulatory certainty and uniformity. In terms of institutional structure, the EU adopts a rigid catalogue of rights limitations as its fundamental model, explicitly enumerating through legislation the applicable scenarios for fair use and statutory exceptions, such as teaching and scientific research. In principle, no expansion beyond the statutory scope is permitted; while member states may introduce detailed provisions within the bounds of the catalogue, they are prohibited from exceeding its limits. The EU copyright system not only safeguards authors' economic interests but also affords robust protection to content creators. Taking France as a prime example, even if the property rights to a work have been transferred, the author retains essential rights over the work's form of expression. Material modifications to the work without the author's consent may still constitute an infringement. By clearly defining relevant rights and their scope of application, the EU copyright system strengthens right holders' control over the modes of work exploitation and reinforces the stability of the copyright regime.

Japan's copyright system has gradually developed a unique orientation centered on promoting technological utilization through legislative reforms. Through multiple amendments to its Copyright Act, Japan has explicitly incorporated "the reproduction, conversion, and utilization of works for the purpose of information analysis" into the scope of statutory licenses or rights limitations. It permits machine learning, data analysis, and model training on protected works, provided that such activities are not conducted for the purpose of enjoying the works' expressions and do not involve direct public dissemination. This institutional design provides a relatively clear legal basis for AI training activities at the legislative level, reducing compliance costs in the data acquisition phase. It also reflects Japan's distinct policy tilt between copyright protection and the development of the AI industry, creating a relaxed policy environment for technological advancement.

China's copyright system, in its overall form, embodies a synthetic absorption of both common law and civil law traditions, featuring both codified statutory norms and room for case-specific judicial discretion. On the one hand, it explicitly enumerates specific categories of fair use through legislation, endowing stakeholders with relatively clear normative expectations under the Copyright Law. On the other hand, it reserves a certain degree of judicial discretion in specific application, allowing courts to conduct interest balancing and render substantive judgments by considering factors such as the nature of the work, the purpose of use, and the scope of impact. This parallel model not only upholds regulatory stability but also reserves appropriate interpretive flexibility for emerging technological scenarios.

Furthermore, national copyright systems also exhibit certain differences in terms of protection scope and duration. U.S. copyright law stipulates that a work must be an original expression fixed in a tangible medium, excluding ideas, facts, or functional elements from protection. The EU adopts a relatively broad interpretation of originality, taking the reflection of the author's intellectual creation as the core criterion for qualifying a work, and affords relatively wider protection to certain applied designs. In terms of the protection of databases and other information compilations, the United States mainly regulates them indirectly through contract law or anti-unfair competition law, whereas the EU has established an independent rights protection mechanism for databases through dedicated directives. China generally adopts a middle-ground stance: it upholds originality as the substantive criterion for work qualification, yet does not impose an unduly high threshold on the degree of originality in judicial practice, instead focusing on further judgments based on specific expressions. In terms of protection duration, the Berne Convention establishes a minimum standard of the author's lifetime plus 50 years after death. Countries and regions including the United States, the EU, and Japan have generally extended this period to 70 years, while setting exception rules for specific types of works. These differences reflect the diverse policy considerations underlying each jurisdiction's copyright system.

At the level of law enforcement and remedies, significant disparities exist among countries in the standards for determining platform liability and duty of care. The United States was among the first to further develop the safe harbor rule and the notice-and-takedown mechanism through case law, providing a liability buffer for technologically neutral platforms. Building on this foundation, the EU has gradually introduced more detailed content supervision obligations for platforms. China, through the parallel operation of administrative law enforcement and judicial adjudication, has gradually established normative responsibilities for platforms in content review and risk control.

The emergence and rise of Generative AI have further amplified the adaptive disparities among national copyright systems. U.S. judicial practice has leveraged the fair use doctrine to carve out considerable leeway for the use of data in AI training. Courts have characterized certain data processing activities as transformative use in relevant cases, as exemplified by the Google Books case, where the U.S. Supreme Court upheld that digitized scanning constitutes transformative use.[19] In contrast, the EU's Artificial Intelligence Act mandates that AI developers disclose the sources of training data, provide right holders with an opt-out mechanism, and imposes more stringent restrictions on data usage. Through the 2018 amendment to its Copyright Act, Japan permits the use of copyrighted materials for non-commercial data mining, provided that such use complies with the three-step test. China has issued a series of laws and policies to regulate data training, explicitly requiring AI service providers to use data legally and respect intellectual property rights. These divergent response approaches reflect the varying institutional orientations of nations in balancing technological development and rights protection.

(2) Common Grounds

Despite the disparities in specific institutions and judicial application across countries, the world's major copyright systems still exhibit notable commonalities in fundamental principles and institutional philosophies. As the cornerstone of global copyright protection, the Berne Convention for the Protection of Literary and Artistic Works has established three core principles, namely national treatment (member states shall provide foreign authors with protection equivalent to that afforded to domestic authors), automatic protection (copyright arises automatically without the need for registration), and minimum standards of protection (the term of

[19] Pamela [19], pp. 20–22.

protection shall be no less than the life of the author plus fifty years), which serve as a reference for the copyright protection systems of all countries.

Such commonalities are first reflected in the criteria for work recognition: countries universally adopt originality as the core requirement for qualifying a work, emphasizing that a work shall embody the author's independent intellectual input and personal expression, without making value judgments on the ideological content itself. The copyright system protects expressions rather than ideas, facts, or methods.[20] The United States has established the "minimum degree of creativity" standard through case adjudication, the EU requires that a work shall reflect the "author's intellectual creation", while both China and Japan emphasize "independent completion with a certain degree of creative expression" in judicial practice. These provisions indicate that all national copyright laws regard whether a work originates from human independent intellectual labor as a prerequisite for obtaining copyright protection, and unanimously exclude ideas, facts, and methods themselves from the scope of copyright protection, thus demarcating the boundary between the public domain and exclusive rights at the institutional level.

Second, copyright systems worldwide generally recognize that copyright has a dual nature encompassing both property rights and moral rights, and their institutional designs are structured around this duality. In terms of property rights, countries take the rights of reproduction, distribution, adaptation, and information network communication as core contents, safeguarding right holders' ability to control the economic exploitation of their works. In terms of moral rights, while countries vary in the intensity of protection and specific content, they generally affirm the statutory status of authors' personal interests in relation to the attribution of authorship and the integrity of their works. The former safeguards creators' economic returns, and the latter upholds their personal dignity, together constituting the balance between economic incentivization and personal respect under the modern copyright system.

In terms of interest adjustment, all national copyright systems impose certain constraints on exclusive rights through the setting of protection terms and rights limitation rules. In terms of protection duration, based on the minimum standards established by the Berne Convention, countries ensure that works will eventually enter the public domain by limiting the duration of rights. In terms of rights limitations, although countries adopt different forms such as fair use, statutory exceptions, or compulsory licensing, their normative orientations are basically consistent: on the premise of not materially prejudicing the legitimate interests of right holders, they permit the necessary use of works in scenarios such as education, scientific research, news dissemination, and public cultural services. The three-step test for permissible uses established by the Berne Convention—i.e., the use shall be confined to certain special cases, shall not conflict with a normal exploitation of the work, and shall not unreasonably prejudice the legitimate interests of the

---

[20] Qi [20], p. 49.

author—also constitutes a common standard for the exception clauses of copyright protection in all countries.[21]

1.4 Intersection of Generative AI and the Copyright System

With the widespread application of Generative AI in the field of content production, the copyright system is no longer confronting the update of a single technical tool, but rather a comprehensive transformation of content generation, dissemination, and utilization models. By virtue of its capacity to generate entirely new content such as texts, images, audio, and video, Generative AI has reshaped the paradigms of creation and cultural production, thereby emerging as one of the most intricate challenges confronting the contemporary copyright system. The intersection of Generative AI and the copyright system manifests itself in three key dimensions: the use of existing works during the training phase, the redefinition of the work attribute of content in the generation phase, and the issues of right boundaries and platform liabilities arising from dissemination and commercialization in the application phase.

1.4.1 Training Phase: Copyright Conflicts Arising from Data Acquisition and Utilization

In the training phase of Generative AI, defining the legality of data acquisition and utilization has become a major focal point of contention in the field of copyright today. Generative AI conducts model training by analyzing and processing massive volumes of data, which typically originate from open networks, commercial copyrighted resources, and user-uploaded content. Although such data are formally input and converted into corpus material comprehensible to the model, the copyright issues entailed in this process cannot be overlooked. Whether unauthorized data utilization constitutes infringement—particularly when the generated content bears a high degree of similarity to the original work—remains legally undefined, and conflicts between Generative AI and the traditional copyright system have gradually come to the fore. Data sources of varying types, ranging from open online resources to copyrighted commercial data, all play critical roles in the training process of Generative AI, yet their legality and compliance remain unresolved challenges. How to balance the need for copyright protection while encouraging technological innovation has become the core issue of current discourse. This issue is not only pertinent to the application of the copyright system, but also bears on how Generative AI technology can develop and be applied within the legal framework, exerting a

[21] Lili [21], pp. 162–163.

profound impact on the interaction and integration of the copyright system and technological innovation.

(1) Data Sources

The training of Generative AI models relies on the continuous input of large-scale datasets, and their training data sources are characterized by diversity and hybridity. Currently, the training corpus of mainstream Generative AI systems is primarily derived from three sources: open web data, commercial copyrighted data, and user-uploaded data.

Open web data constitute the most fundamental and voluminous data source. Open web data refer to structured or unstructured texts publicly available on internet platforms, including but not limited to written texts, images, audio-visual content, and source codes.[22] Their shared characteristic is open accessibility to the public, and they are scattered across a highly fragmented cyberspace. Through continuous crawling by automated programs, such data can be systematically collected in a short period and transformed into corpus resources for model training. For this reason, open web data are often regarded in practice as a low-threshold, large-scale data source. However, it is crucial to clarify that the public accessibility of a work does not automatically mean that it has entered the public domain. A substantial amount of online content still constitutes textual, visual, musical, and audio-visual works protected by copyright law. The presumption that such data can be freely used for model training simply because they exist in an open online environment will give rise to legal risks.

Commercial copyrighted data, as a training data source, have relatively clear right boundaries, and their associated risks are more concentrated. Such data mainly include licensed image libraries, music libraries, film and television material databases, as well as academic journal and professional literature databases. Unlike open web data, such data are usually subject to a rigorous authorization management system; their ownership of rights is clearly defined, and their scope and methods of use are generally constrained by both contractual clauses and copyright law norms. The use of commercial copyrighted data is not automatically permitted, but is predicated on the payment of consideration and the acquisition of authorization. If such data are directly incorporated into the training process of Generative AI without obtaining authorization, the resulting infringement risks are often clearly identifiable, and judicial determination of liability is also more straightforward. Precisely for this reason, the existence of commercial copyrighted data renders the training activities of Generative AI inevitably intertwined with the established copyright system.

User-uploaded data have gradually evolved into an increasingly important source of training data in recent years. User-uploaded data refer to content actively input by users during their use of Generative AI products, including dialogue texts, image materials, audio files, and program codes. In conversational models, a vast amount

[22] Taotao [22], p. 180.

of human-machine interaction content is recorded by the system during use and utilized for subsequent model optimization and retraining. User-uploaded data often involve both the copyright held by users over the input content and the usage rights obtained by platforms based on service agreements. Different platforms typically stipulate the retention, processing, and reuse of input content through user agreements, privacy policies, or data usage terms. Nevertheless, significant room for controversy remains regarding these terms, particularly in relation to the scope of authorization, ownership of rights, and the authenticity of users' expressed intentions. Meanwhile, the sources of the content input by users may themselves involve third-party works, rendering the acquisition and utilization of such training data an even more complex overlapping landscape.

(2) Core Conflicts

In the training phase of Generative AI, massive volumes of data are continuously incorporated into model training without the permission of right holders. Whether this act constitutes "reproduction" within the meaning of copyright law, and thus potentially constitutes an infringement of the reproduction right, has become the most central legal controversy in the training phase. According to traditional copyright law theory, the unauthorized reproduction of a protected work, where such reproduction does not fall within statutory exceptions such as fair use, constitutes infringement in principle. Whether the training act amounts to "reproduction" under copyright law is the primary focus of disputes surrounding the ownership of training data. During training, the model is required to digitally read, store, disassemble, and recombine original works. While this process serves the purpose of technical learning, it still objectively presupposes the incorporation of works into the system. Even if these works are not presented in their complete original form in the final generated content, their reading and retention during the training phase may still be deemed as the utilization of the entire work or its substantial parts. Such "reproduction for learning purposes" has no direct counterpart in the traditional copyright framework, making it difficult to reach a clear determination under the traditional copyright system. This exposes the traditional standards for identifying copyright subjects to the risk of technical deconstruction.[23]

From an objective procedural perspective, during training, Generative AI needs to conduct large-scale digital reading and storage of original works, and transform the works into computable weight structures for neural networks through tokenization, vectorization, feature extraction, and parameter fitting. Although what the model ultimately generates consists of parameter weights rather than the original works themselves, and these weights do not possess expressiveness directly perceptible to humans, the aforementioned training process still objectively presupposes the digital reproduction of the entire work or its substantial parts. This type of reproduction for the purpose of technical learning has no exact counterpart in the current copyright law system, thereby triggering disputes over the application of the

[23] Taotao [23], p. 183.

reproduction right. In this regard, the crux does not lie in whether the training act technically results in the reproduction of the work, but in whether such reproduction exceeds the boundaries of permissible utilization under copyright law and materially impairs the interest structure of right holders.

In terms of legal evaluation, the reproduction right is not an absolute right; its scope of exercise is always subject to the influence of public interests, technological development, and market structures. Determining whether reproduction during the training phase constitutes infringement cannot be based solely on the formal criterion of "whether a reproduction act exists", but should instead be a comprehensive assessment considering the purpose of use, manner of use, scale of use, and the impact on the market of the original work. On the one hand, model training is not intended to directly disseminate works to the public, and the intermediate reproductions generated during the training process are distinctly instrumental and procedural in nature. On the other hand, the model's capabilities themselves have a clear commercial orientation, and the fruits of training ultimately enter the market in the form of products and generate economic benefits, meaning that the reproductions made during training are not divorced from the market structure.

Proceeding from the basic provisions of the copyright system, the reproduction right is not an absolute right; its scope of exercise is perpetually influenced by public interests and technological development. Whether the act of reproducing data by Generative AI during the training phase constitutes infringement cannot be judged merely by the formal standard of "whether a reproduction act exists", but requires a comprehensive consideration of the purpose of use, manner of use, scope of use, and the impact on the market of the original work.

Model training is not aimed at directly disseminating works to the public, and the intermediate reproductions formed during the training process are characterized by obvious instrumentality and procedurality. The training process is essentially a technical utilization, whose purpose is to extract implicit knowledge such as linguistic structures and semantic relationships, rather than to provide materials for human reading or appreciation.[24] On the other hand, however, such reproductions for training purposes are not divorced from the market. When the model's capabilities have a clear commercial orientation, the outcomes of training will eventually enter the market and generate economic returns. In this sense, although the reproductions made during the model training phase do not directly substitute for the consumption of the original works, they may participate in competition in the content market in other forms. Particularly when the model can stably generate content of a specific style, type, or structure, the original works relied upon for training are in fact incorporated into the value conversion process. The indirect utilization mediated by the model's capabilities establishes a structural continuity between data acquisition in the model training phase and traditional infringing reproduction acts, rather than a complete disconnect.

[24] Cheng [24], p. 7.

Furthermore, although in terms of outcomes, model weights are not equivalent to the original works and in principle do not possess "expressiveness" directly perceptible to humans, under specific conditions—such as insufficient training samples, overfitting of model parameters, or the abnormal amplification of the weights of specific samples—the model may still form a memory of certain training samples. As a result, during the generation phase, it may output content that is highly similar to the original works in terms of expression structure, plot arrangement, or linguistic style, thereby constituting de facto indirect reproduction. In such cases, the act of reproduction during the training phase may also carry the risk of infringement.

The key to determining whether reproduction during the training phase constitutes infringement does not depend on whether the model "stores the original text of the work", but on whether such reproduction constitutes a material intervention in the economic exploitation methods of the work. If the training act remains at the level of technical learning and does not cause identifiable damage to the market value of the original work, it should not be deemed as infringement. Conversely, if the training act, in terms of scale, scope, and specific usage effects, materially substitutes the potential market for a specific work, then the reproduction act may fall within the regulatory scope of the reproduction right.

1.4.2 Generation Phase: Copyright Qualification of AI-Generated Content

With the widespread application of Generative AI technology, copyright issues have become increasingly prominent, particularly regarding the copyright qualification of Artificial Intelligence Generated Content (AIGC). Generative AI can automatically generate various types of content such as texts, images, audio, and videos based on user input instructions, and is widely used in fields including advertising creation and design production. The generation process has sparked legal disputes over "originality" and the constitution of a work. The current copyright system generally requires works to embody the independent intellectual achievements of creators. In contrast, AIGC often does not directly reflect human creative intent and is entirely generated automatically by machines based on algorithms. However, the generation process is not completely divorced from human participation: users gradually guide the direction and expression of the generated content through prompts. This human-machine collaborative creation method means that AIGC may be deemed a "work" under copyright law, thereby triggering more complex legal issues regarding the attribution of rights.

(1) Focal Points of Dispute

AIGC refers to content forms such as texts, images, audio, or videos automatically generated by AI systems based on user input instructions, supported by algorithmic rules and data structures. After completing training, Generative AI outputs content such as texts, images, and audio in response to user input instructions, which are widely applied in practical scenarios including advertising, content creation, design production, and information services. Conflicts between AI and the copyright system are no longer confined to the technical level, but have transformed from a potential state to observable and evaluable practical institutional issues. Among these, whether AIGC meets the requirement of "originality" and thus satisfies the conditions for constituting a work has become the core focal point of dispute in the generation phase.

From the perspective of work recognition, the current copyright system universally adopts "originality" as the core criterion for determining whether something constitutes a work. Originality does not require the work to possess a high degree of novelty or artistic value objectively, but emphasizes that the work shall embody the minimum threshold of creative expression made by a natural person based on independent intellectual activity. Whether it is the "minimum degree of creativity" emphasized by the common law system or the "intellectual creation achievement" stressed by the civil law system, the two are highly consistent in normative connotation, with their common foundation lying in the requirement that a work must be traceable to the intellectual activity of a specific natural person.

Models do not understand the meaning of the content they generate, nor do they possess the ability to make value judgments or choices. The generation process is merely a technical process of combining, transforming, and reconstructing existing information. Although this process is highly complex and exhibits uncertainty in outcomes, its generation logic operates within a statistically predefined framework by algorithms and does not form a creative act centered on expressive will in the legal sense. Therefore, in cases of purely automated generation—i.e., when the formation of content is completely accomplished by the system without any identifiable human intellectual intervention—AIGC generally fails to meet the traditional criteria for originality under current copyright law, and the justification for including it in the scope of work protection is relatively weak. Judicial and administrative practices in various countries also generally adopt a negative copyright stance toward "AI-generated results without human intervention," with the fundamental reason being that such results cannot be attributed to the creative act of a natural person.

In practical applications, however, the generation process of AIGC is often not completely separated from human participation. Users define generation objectives through prompts, impose initial constraints on the generation direction, continuously adjust instruction content during multi-round interactions, and screen, retry, and modify output results. This causes the generated content to gradually deviate from the model's initial random output state and present a more stable and clear expressive orientation. In such cases, the focus of thc copyright system shifts from whether AI possesses creativity to whether the user has invested intellectually recognizable activity throughout the generation process. If the user's prompt design is limited to simple instructions and the generated result is completely completed automatically by the system, the content still cannot be deemed the intellectual creation achievement of a natural person. However, if the user continuously guides the generation process, screens, selects, and processes the output content to reflect their creative objectives and personalized choices, the final result should be regarded as the user's work.[25] Whether AIGC constitutes a work does not depend on the technology itself, but rather on whether humans have completed legally recognizable substantive creation during the generation process. The mainstream view also holds that AI is a tool for humans to create works, and advocates that the determination of whether its generated content constitutes a work should be based on objective results.[26]

Whether AIGC constitutes a work cannot be judged by the single criterion of "whether it is generated by AI." The key lies not in the technology itself, but in whether humans have completed legally recognizable substantive creation during the generation process. In this sense, Generative AI is more akin to a highly automated creative tool. Whether its output results fall into the category of "works" protected by copyright law depends on whether the tool is embedded in the creative activities of natural persons and leaves identifiable intellectual traces in the final result. When addressing this focal point of dispute, it is necessary to return to the traditional judgment framework of originality, and conduct a case-by-case evaluation of the work attribute of AIGC based on objective results, combined with the degree of human intervention and capability—rather than making a one-size-fits-all affirmation or negation.

(2) Derivative Issues

On the premise that AIGC is deemed a work, the issue of right attribution naturally arises. Practical discussions usually involve four potential subjects: the AI system for training data, the original copyright holders, the model developers, and the users who directly generate content using the system. The AIGC generation process involves the participation of multiple elements including algorithm systems, data resources, and user instructions, which means the creation of the work no longer corresponds to a single subject, thus rendering the attribution of rights relatively complicated.

First, it can be clearly affirmed that AI itself does not possess legal personality and cannot become a subject of rights and obligations. Therefore, the generated content cannot be attributed to the generation system itself, and the system thus cannot qualify as a right holder in the sense of copyright law.[27] Both the provisions on civil subjects in civil law and the concept of authors in copyright law require that a right holder must be capable of performing creative acts, bearing legal consequences, and enjoying the benefits derived therefrom. Generative AI exists merely as a highly sophisticated information processing tool; its output does not stem from its own value judgments or subjective will, and thus cannot constitute "independent creation" in the legal sense. The prevailing view also generally regards AI as a

[25] Guobin [25], p. 15.

[26] Lixian and Yonglin [26], p. 171.

[27] Xiaoqing and Yun [27], pp. 16–17.

technical tool without legal personality, meaning AIGC cannot be attributed to the Generative AI system itself, and the attribution of rights must be resolved among natural persons or legal persons. Conversely, however, some viewpoints further advocate that AI should be deemed an independent right holder through legislative techniques, allowing it to directly enjoy the copyright of the works it generates. This approach draws on the legal fiction doctrine, attempting to formally resolve the issue of AIGC copyright attribution by endowing AI with "legal personality", and to provide a legal basis for the circulation and utilization of generated content.[28] This proposition can avoid the right uncertainty caused by repeated games between developers, users, and platforms, but AI does not have the capacity to bear liabilities, and its "rights" still need to be exercised by humans in practice, making the fictional subject inevitably a mere formality. Furthermore, directly vesting rights in a technical system without subjective consciousness may easily lead to the instrumentalization and hollowing-out of the copyright system, which is difficult to gain widespread recognition under the current copyright legal framework.

On the premise of denying AI as a right holder, the attribution of rights must be determined among actual natural persons or legal persons. Around this issue, different viewpoints have gradually emerged in theory and practice, such as the developer doctrine, the data provider doctrine, and the user doctrine.

The view that attributes rights to developers focuses on emphasizing that the model's capabilities stem from projects such as model architecture and parameter training, holding that developers exercise decisive control over the generation mechanism itself. However, this view ignores the fact that the specific expression of the generated results is not preset during the development phase, but is generated in real time triggered by specific user instructions; developers do not perform specific creative acts on individual generated results. The output of generated results is neither preset nor controlled by developers, and there is no direct relationship of control between them. If developers could obtain the copyright of all generated content merely by providing the technology, it would not only lead to excessive concentration of rights in the hands of developers, but also weaken the enthusiasm for creation.[29]

The view that attributes rights to the copyright holders of training data attempts to establish the right basis for generated content from the perspective of content sources, arguing that AIGC is an algorithmic extension of existing works. However, such a determination is generally untenable in law, because AIGC generated results are the recombination and transformation of multi-source data in probabilistic models, which do not constitute the reproduction or substitution of specific works, nor can they form a corresponding relationship with any original work in terms of expression structure. If the original authors were to be endowed with the right basis for subsequent unspecified generated content merely because their works were included in the training corpus, it would not only lead to the unlimited expansion of

---

[28] Guanbin [28], pp. 145–146.

[29] Ping [29], pp. 23–24.

right boundaries, but also fundamentally undermine the basic requirement of the copyright system regarding the certainty of the object of rights.

In comparison, the view that rights should be attributed to users is more practically feasible and more consistent with the logic of the copyright system that takes creative acts as the basis for right allocation. Users define generation objectives through prompts, restrict the direction of expression, continuously adjust input parameters, and screen, select, and post-process output results during multi-round generation, exerting a direct impact on the final output. Their acts are closest to participatory creation in the traditional sense, and are thus most easily incorporated into the scope regulated by the current copyright system. AI is better understood as a highly sophisticated creative tool rather than an independent creative subject. As long as users invest legally recognizable intellectual creation in the generation process, making the generated content reflect clear human will in structure or expression, there is an institutional basis for incorporating it into the category of works by natural persons and vesting the copyright in them.[30]

It should be further pointed out, however, that even though the "user attribution doctrine" is more reasonable in normative terms, it has not completely resolved the practical conflicts arising from the attribution of AIGC rights. Platforms usually impose restrictions on the use, distribution, reuse, and commercial development of generated content through user agreements, service terms, and API authorization rules, thus actually exerting a certain influence over the generated content. Meanwhile, the high degree of automation in the generation process and the instability of output results make users' control over the final product phased and uneven, and their creative contributions vary significantly across different scenarios, which further increases the difficulty of determining the attribution of AIGC rights.

Overall, the issues of work recognition and right attribution triggered by AIGC have in fact shaken the provisions of the traditional copyright system regarding works and authors. The automation and uncertainty of the generation mechanism have rendered creative acts a multi-subject, multi-level composite form. On the other hand, platforms as technology providers have significantly weakened the ability of a single subject to control the creative content. Against this background, the work attribute and right attribution of AIGC are no longer a matter of applying a single clause, but involve multiple issues including the determination of works, originality, and right attribution.

[30] Ping [29], pp. 23–24.

1.4.3 Utilization Phase: Right Boundaries for the Dissemination and Commercial Use of AIGC

When AI-generated content is widely applied in commercial scenarios such as advertising, product design, brand marketing, and film production, the relevant legal issue shifts to whether it can be used legally. Whether users may directly put AIGC into commercial use and whether further authorization is required have become the core practical controversies in the utilization phase. At the same time, infringement risks are not only associated with users. Since generated content relies on models and services provided by platforms, whether AI service providers can still be regarded as mere technical intermediaries and whether they shall bear corresponding liabilities for users' infringing acts have gradually become unavoidable key issues in judicial practice and regulatory discussions.

(1) Practical Controversies

When AIGC enters the phase of dissemination and commercial exploitation, its legal risks are no longer confined to the technical level, but further evolve into practical disputes surrounding dissemination and commercial use. New legal issues emerge when users apply generated content to commercial scenarios including advertising, product design, brand packaging, and film creation. In this phase, practical controversies are concentrated on whether users are entitled to commercially exploit AIGC and whether corresponding authorization is required.

The core issues concerning the right boundaries of AIGC do not lie in the technical aspects of Generative AI, but in two questions: first, whether the generated content itself constitutes a work within the meaning of copyright law; second, whether the content infringes on the prior rights of others. If AIGC is deemed a work due to the user's input of substantive creativity, it may in principle enjoy complete right attributes in terms of dissemination and commercial use. However, this scope of rights is not subject to unlimited expansion, but is always restricted by the boundaries of others' existing rights. It is only valid when the generated content itself does not constitute an infringement on others' works, trademarks, portraits, or other prior rights.

Within the framework of the existing copyright system, whether authorization is required for commercial use first depends on whether the generated content itself constitutes a work under copyright law. If the relevant content is recognized as a work due to the user's substantive creative input, the user, as the right holder, shall in principle be entitled to reproduce, distribute, adapt, and commercially exploit the content without needing to obtain separate permission from others. Nevertheless, this conclusion is not automatically valid; its validity is premised on the generated content being free from right defects and not encroaching on the scope of others' prior rights. If the generated content is substantially similar to existing works in terms of style, structure, and expression, or has reached the level of substituting the original works, its commercial use may still exceed the permissible boundaries of fair use under copyright law. Therefore, publishing AI-generated content without the authorization of the original authors may expose users to legal risks of infringing on the original authors' reproduction rights.[31]

Furthermore, commercial uses such as advertising and product design are inherently highly distinctive and transmissible. Once generated content is used for product packaging, brand promotion, or public distribution, its impact on the market is no longer limited to information expression, but directly enters the realm of market competition. In such cases, whether the generated content has independent expressiveness and is sufficiently distinguishable from existing works becomes an important criterion for judging whether separate authorization is required. The generation method cannot automatically grant the legitimacy of "free commercial use"; once generated content is used for profit-making purposes, it still needs to undergo the same standard of right review as traditional creative achievements. In addition, generated content may also involve the names and portraits of specific natural persons, or the logos, goodwill, and commercial decorations of enterprises, thus falling into the adjustment scope of personality rights law and trademark law. Compared with non-commercial personal use, commercial exploitation inherently entails a higher intensity of legal review and more stringent authorization requirements. However, in the practice of AIGC utilization, the source of rights is highly uncertain, and generated content is often difficult to trace back to any specific original work. Users are also unable to accurately identify which work the generated results "resemble" or "borrow from", making it practically impossible to obtain clear authorization. This renders seeking permission from right holders generally unfeasible in practice and objectively exacerbates the compliance risks of AIGC commercial use.

Second, the right boundaries for the use of AI-generated content are also influenced by platforms. Most Generative AI service providers stipulate the permissible scope of utilization of generated content through user agreements. For example, some platforms allow users to freely conduct commercial use under certain conditions; others explicitly permit users to commercially exploit AIGC under specific circumstances while imposing restrictions on uses involving the images of public figures, specific commercial logos, high-risk industries, or highly stylized outputs. Platform user agreements mean that whether AI-generated content can be legally used for commercial purposes is to a considerable extent directly affected by platform rules, and is no longer solely determined by the provisions of copyright law. However, while platform authorization formally provides users with a basis for using AIGC, it is essentially a contractual licensing arrangement rather than an exclusion of third parties' prior rights. Therefore, even if a user has obtained authorization at the platform level, it does not automatically mean that their use is completely legal under the law. Platform authorization only addresses the division of rights between users and platforms, and cannot replace the prudent review of others' prior rights. Once the generated content actually encroaches on others' works, trademarks, or personality rights and interests, it may still constitute legal infringement even if it complies with platform rules.

[31] Yuchen [30], p. 101.

It can thus be concluded that, in the phase of dissemination and commercial exploitation, whether authorization is required for generated content does not depend on whether it is AI-generated, but returns to the core issues concerned by the traditional copyright system: whether the content constitutes a work, whether it encroaches on others' prior rights, whether it exceeds the scope of fair use, and whether it complies with existing use license arrangements. The AI generation mechanism is merely a technical path for content creation, and cannot automatically alter the basic judgment on right boundaries in the process of commercial exploitation.

(2) Platform Liability

When users disseminate or commercially exploit AI-generated content, thereby triggering the risk of infringing others' copyrights, whether platforms shall bear liability for users' infringing acts has long been a core topic in technology governance.[32] Unlike traditional internet service providers, Generative AI service providers do not merely passively store or transmit user-uploaded content; instead, they directly participate in the content generation process through algorithm systems, which renders their legal status in infringement assessment more complicated.

From the perspective of user utilization, whether AIGC can be legally used for commercial purposes first depends on whether the generated content itself constitutes a work under copyright law and whether it has right defects. If AIGC is recognized as a protected work due to the user's substantive creative input, the user, as the right holder, shall in principle be entitled to reproduce, distribute, adapt, and commercially exploit it. However, this right is not automatically valid; its legality is still subject to two constraints: first, whether the generated content encroaches on others' prior rights; second, whether the platform service agreement imposes restrictions on commercial exploitation.

When users commit infringing acts by using AIGC, whether platforms constitute infringement or only bear liability based on the notice-and-takedown rule often becomes a key issue in judicial proceedings. If infringing content is completely uploaded and disseminated by users, while the AI service provider only provides technical intermediary services without conducting substantive editing, selection, or promotion of specific content, the safe harbor rule in the field of information network dissemination shall apply in principle. As long as the platform fulfills its necessary obligation of notification and promptly takes measures such as deletion and link-breaking upon receiving a claim from the right holder, it usually does not bear direct liability for the consequences of the user's infringement.[33]

In the application scenarios of Generative AI, however, infringing content is not completely uploaded by users, but generated in real time by the platform model based on user instructions. This establishes a closer generative connection between the platform and the infringing content. Under such circumstances, whether

[32] Ling [31], p. 5.

[33] Zhiwei [32], pp. 64–65.

platforms can still fully apply the traditional safe harbor rule has become a key focal point of dispute in theory and practice. According to general rules, the crux of whether a platform shall bear liability lies in whether it has "actual knowledge or constructive knowledge" of the infringement risk and whether it has in fact exerted a material influence on the generation and dissemination of infringing content.

If a platform only provides a general-purpose generation tool without conducting targeted intervention on user input and output results, has pre-set copyright risk prompts and usage restrictions, and promptly takes necessary disposal measures upon receiving claims from right holders, it can usually claim exemption from liability in accordance with the safe harbor rule in the field of information network dissemination. It will be deemed as providing neutral technical services, and shall not be presumed to constitute joint infringement. The safe harbor rule retains the scenario of "actual knowledge" but narrows down the scope of "constructive knowledge": courts can only presume that the service provider has knowledge of the infringing act when it "knows any facts that clearly indicate the existence of infringing activities".[34] If the platform has knowledge of the infringement risk but still condones it, or even amplifies the dissemination effect of infringing content through recommendation, monetization, and other means, its legal evaluation will change accordingly. For example, if the platform continuously guides users to generate content that is highly similar to the style or structure of specific works through template guidance, style recommendation, content optimization suggestions, etc. Or, in cases where right holders have repeatedly claimed infringement risks, the platform still makes no adjustments to relevant functions, but instead expands the dissemination scope of infringing content through traffic distribution, commercial monetization, and other mechanisms, then its act will no longer be confined to pure technical support. Its legal status may shift from a neutral service provider to a joint participant, thereby bearing corresponding joint tort liability.

Whether an AI service provider shall bear liability does not depend on whether it directly created the infringing content, but on whether it has incorporated the infringing act into its predictable and controllable business activities through its own system mechanism, operation mode, and revenue arrangement. When an AI service provider has actual control over the infringement risk but still allows relevant content to be continuously generated and enter the field of dissemination and commercial circulation, its legal status may shift from a neutral service provider to a participant in the infringing act.

Currently, most Generative AI platforms stipulate through user agreement clauses that users shall enjoy the right to use the generated content, but platforms often explicitly disclaim any warranty for the legality of the generated content through exemption clauses, and require users to bear the infringement risks arising from their use of the content independently. This risk allocation through contractual mechanisms formally entrusts the commercial exploitation space of AIGC to users, but in essence also transfers potential legal liabilities to users, making them the

---

[34] Guobin [33], p. 141.

direct bearers of copyright risks. User agreements have certain validity within civil legal relations, but cannot naturally override the determination of infringement liability under copyright law. Even if the platform "transfers" risks to users through clause agreements, it cannot be exempted from the statutory liability that it should bear when objectively participating in infringement.

To sum up, the continuous disputes triggered by Generative AI in the field of copyright are not fundamentally due to the difficulty in applying a single rule, but to the fact that the technical operation mode of Generative AI is deeply embedded in the entire process of works from being used to being reproduced, and then to being disseminated and commercially exploited. The use of existing works in the training phase has led to conflicts over reproduction right infringement; the generation phase has given rise to disputes over the scope of works and authors; the utilization phase has resulted in right conflicts and platform liability issues centering on dissemination and commercial use. It is in this continuous process that multiple contradictions between Generative AI and the copyright system have been constantly amplified, which also lays a realistic foundation for subsequent institutional responses.

References

1. Xiaofeng C, Xibin S (2024) Research on the impacts, challenges and countermeasures of generative artificial intelligence reshaping the Sci-tech journal industry[J]. Chinese Journal of Scientific and Technical Periodicals 7:890
2. Hechuan Y, Yanhong W (2025) Copyright risks of generative artificial intelligence and its regulatory path[J]. Chuanbo yu Banquan 13:106
3. Tong Z, Guowei S, Weiliang L et al (2025) Research on generative artificial intelligence technology empowering the development of digital economy[J]. Inner Mongolia Science Technology & Economy 5:98–99
4. Yao W, Shengli L (2023) Copyright risks of generative artificial intelligence and their countermeasures—from the perspective of ChatGPT[J]. Hainan Finance 10:49–58
5. Zubing L (2024) On the copyright dilemmas and resolution paths of generative artificial intelligence using pre-existing works[J]. Journal of Information Resources Management 14:149
6. Jingwei L et al (2023) Beyond chatting with ChatGPT: opportunities and challenges of ultra-large pre-trained models[J]. Acta Automatica Sinica 4:709–710
7. Fengge J, Haifang Y (2025) Legal regulation of generative artificial intelligence: from the perspective of technology and human-machine relationships[J]. Seeking Truth 52:125–126
8. Huiyuan D (2025) Identification of liability subjects for copyright infringement by generative artificial intelligence[J]. Electronics Intellectual Property 17
9. Zhen Z, Yiwen Z, Chi L (2025) The embedding of generative artificial intelligence into social governance: internal mechanisms, risk patterns and regulatory paths[J]. Journal of Dialectics of Nature 47:110
10. Zhiwen L (2025) The qualification of generative AI outputs and the liability rules thereof in copyright law. Law Science 6:132–133
11. Wen D (2023) Research on the Copyrightability of generative AI content represented by ChatGPT[J]. Political Science and Law 9:87–88
12. Taotao W (2025a) Infringement risks and regulatory paths of generative artificial intelligence training data[J]. Chinese Journal of Law 4:180

13. Linghan Z, Jianjun Y, Yuheng W et al (2025) Continuations and new chapters: an annual observation of China's AI rule of law research in 2024[J]. Journal of Law Application 3:159
14. Ge Z, Guobin C, Qian W et al (2024) Are AI-generated contents (AIGC) protected by copyright law?[J]. China Law Review 3:5
15. Ping Z (2023) Breakthrough innovation of generative artificial intelligence requires sound law and good governance——taking the legitimacy of data training as an example[J]. New Economy Leader 8:27
16. Xiang L (2024) Does the "contribution" protected by copyright law come from the question or the answer? — reflections on the Copyrightability of AI-generated content[J]. Nanjing University Law Journal 5:151–152
17. Qi X (2011) The legal structure of the copyright incentive mechanism[M]. Renmin University of China Press, Beijing, p 236
18. Kaixin Z (2024) Research on generative artificial intelligence and the protection of copyrighted works[J]. Publishing Research 7:85
19. Pamela S (2021) Speaking text and data Mining of in-Copyright Works: is it legal? [J]. Commun ACM 64(11):20–22
20. Qi X (2025) Solutions to frontier disputes in China's copyright law[J]. SJTU Law Review 5:49
21. Lili W (2025) The application choice of copyright limitation Systems in Generative Artificial Intelligence Data Training[J]. Journal of Political Science and Law 5:162–163
22. Taotao W (2025b) Infringement risks and regulatory paths of generative artificial intelligence training data[J]. Journal of Qinghai Minzu University (Social Sciences) 51:180
23. Taotao W (2025c) Infringement risks and regulatory paths of generative artificial intelligence training data[J]. Chinese Journal of Law 4:183
24. Cheng L (2025) Copyright protection for generative artificial intelligence data training and its international experience[J]. Chongqing Social Sciences 7:7
25. Guobin C (2023) The user's original contribution in AI-generated works[J]. China Copyright 6:15
26. Lixian C, Yonglin L (2023) Work recognition and copyright attribution of generative AI—taking the application scenarios of ChatGPT's works as an example[J]. Journal of Shandong University (Philosophy and Social Sciences) 4:171
27. Xiaoqing F, Yun S (2023) Research on copyright issues of generative artificial intelligence[J]. China Copyright 2:16–17
28. Guanbin S (2018) On the copyright protection of works created by intelligent robots——from the perspective of the subject qualification of intelligent robots[J]. Oriental Law 3:145–146
29. Ping Z (2024) Institutional responses to copyright issues of generative artificial intelligence[J]. Nanfang Media Research 5:23–24
30. Yuchen Y (2025) Research on publishers' reasonable duty of care against the background of generative AI applications[J]. Editorial Friend 9:101
31. Ling H (2019) Legal liability of artificial intelligence from the perspective of platforms[J]. SJTU Law Review 3:5
32. Zhiwei Y (2025) The liability exemption system for generative AI search service providers in case of infringement[J]. Global Law Review 6:64–65
33. Guobin C (2013) Reshaping the joint tort liability system for internet service providers[J]. Chinese Journal of Law 4:141

Chapter 2
Copyright Compliance Issues of Generative AI Training Data

2.1 Sources and Characteristics of Generative AI Training Data

Training data refers to annotated or benchmark datasets used to train machine learning models.[1] For generative AI, training data consists of diverse datasets employed to train its models. The sources and formats of such data collectively shape the landscape of generative AI, which serves as the factual basis for analyzing copyright compliance. Given that training data typically comes from multiple sources and includes vast volumes of texts, images, audio, and other works, it often carries inherent copyright infringement risks.

2.1.1 Classification of Primary Sources of Training Data

Legitimacy of data sources is critical to ensuring training data compliance and constitutes a core element in determining copyright infringement risks in the AI sector. The generative capabilities of AI models rely heavily on iterative training with massive, high-quality datasets. Accordingly, Article 7 of China's Interim Measures for the Administration of Generative Artificial Intelligence Services explicitly stipulates that generative AI service providers must lawfully conduct pre-training, fine-tuning, and other data processing activities using legally sourced data and base models, and must not infringe upon others' legally protected intellectual property rights. This provision aims to regulate the legitimacy of training

[1] Article 23(5), Provisions on the Administration of Deep Synthesis of Internet Information Services.

L. Cheng, *Copyright Issues Related to Generative Artificial Intelligence (AI)*, Artificial Intelligence and the Rule of Law,
https://doi.org/10.1007/978-981-95-8781-0_2

data sources for providers, a key focus in the current generative AI landscape. Classifying training data sources facilitates standardized data governance, underpins compliant usage, and ensures the legality of generative AI outputs. Based on acquisition methods and usage rights, generative AI training data can be categorized into three primary types.

Type 1: Publicly Accessible Data

This is the preferred source for model developers. Publicly accessible data refers to datasets that can be freely obtained and used through open channels without requiring special authorization. Common acquisition methods include web crawling of publicly available web content, social media posts (e.g., Twitter, Facebook), digitized public library collections, and open-source repositories (e.g., Wikipedia), which are then compiled into training corpora. Characterized by scale, diversity, comprehensiveness, and breadth, this data covers virtually all domains and formats (text, images, audio, etc.). However, public accessibility does not equate to unrestricted free use. Such datasets often include works in the public domain alongside copyrighted works used without authorization. While browsing such content may be permissible, incorporating copyrighted materials into training datasets without consent typically poses significant copyright infringement risks.

Type 2: Licensed Data

Licensed data is obtained with explicit permission from rights holders via contracts, subscriptions, or purchases. Examples include copyright libraries acquired from collective management organizations (e.g., China Audio-Video Copyright Association), specialized databases, and authorized content from platforms such as Zhihu and Getty Images through formal agreements. Its core strengths lie in compliance and high quality: it generally eliminates infringement risks during acquisition and usage, avoids "junk data" and data contamination through curation, enhances domain-specific accuracy and reliability of models, addresses gaps in the professionalism of public data, and improves the quality of generated outputs.

Type 3: Unauthorized Data

Unauthorized data is acquired or used without proper authorization or in violation of legal provisions. It encompasses "grey data" such as copyrighted works uploaded by users without permission, pirated content downloaded from underground libraries, copyrighted materials procured from darknet platforms, and foreign copyrighted works not distributed in China. Marked by opacity and confidentiality, using such data exposes AI developers to clear infringement liability. Additionally, it often contains low-quality or irrelevant data, leading to data contamination, which in turn causes models to generate misinformation and severely disrupts information order.

2.1.2 *Technical Characteristics of Training Data and Copyright Challenges*

The data sources, technical principles, and training objectives of generative AI language models determine their core technical characteristics: massiveness, hybridity, and opacity.

(1) Massiveness

The core goal of a generative AI system is to learn linguistic patterns and knowledge rules from massive datasets, thereby generating content comparable to human creations. This objective dictates that only when the scale of training data reaches a certain threshold can the model move beyond basic data integration and exhibit complex capabilities such as logical reasoning and content creation. The training datasets of generative AI include digitized textual works, as well as digitized content re-encoded into machine-readable formats. These datasets boast wide-ranging sources, enormous scale, and diverse types—encompassing text, images, audio, video, and more—enabling the model to generate content with higher accuracy and relevance.

As reported, the training data volume of a single large language model can reach the trillion-character level. For instance, according to official disclosures from OpenAI, GPT-3 has 175 billion parameters, while the training data volume of GPT-4 exceeds 13 trillion tokens. Baidu's ERNIE Bot is trained on data including tens of billions of daily voice interaction records, billions of search and image data points, trillion-level web page data, and a knowledge graph containing 550 billion factual entries.[2] Such a colossal data scale inherently gives rise to copyright legitimacy issues regarding data collection and usage.

From a legislative intent perspective, China's Copyright Law grants exclusive rights such as reproduction and adaptation to copyright holders, aiming to incentivize creation and boost the development and prosperity of socialist culture and science. Under current legal provisions, generative AI service providers should obtain prior permission from copyright holders and pay remuneration for the use of copyrighted works in training. Unauthorized use of copyrighted content—such as training models with others' original works without consent, or crawling data through illegal means like violating Robots protocols or bypassing anti-crawling measures—will expose subsequent training and generated content to copyright infringement risks.

However, traditional licensing models face obvious obstacles in the context of generative AI training. The massiveness of training data means that copyright holders are numerous and geographically dispersed; additionally, the rights holders of some works remain unidentified. Identifying all copyright holders and obtaining

[2] Sun Qiru. Baidu Releases ERNIE Bot; Robin Li: Large Language Models Cannot Be Rushed. Beijing Daily, March 16, 2023. https://xinwen.bjd.com.cn/content/s6412ca35e4b03a6b6ed-d3af8.html.

individual authorizations is extremely difficult and inefficient. Furthermore, securing comprehensive authorization would increase model training costs, squeezing the survival space of small and medium-sized enterprises. When training costs far outweigh benefits, the enthusiasm of AI developers will be severely dampened. At present, judicial cases involving the unauthorized use of copyrighted works for large model training are frequent, such as multiple authors suing Anthropic and Meta for copyright infringement. This issue demands urgent resolution.

(2) Hybridity

Training data is also characterized by hybridity. As mentioned earlier, the training data of generative AI is not sourced from a single channel but is widely collected from web pages, social media, open-source libraries, proprietary databases, etc. This collection method directly results in the hybrid nature of training data, which is mainly reflected in two aspects: content hybridity and compliance hybridity.

First, model training usually requires converting collected text, images, videos, and other content into a unified, machine-readable format to form a dataset. Such datasets contain both structured and unstructured data, as well as high-quality content and "junk" data. Second, in terms of data compliance, the initial stage of model training adopts self-supervised learning, where developers only need to "feed" the dataset to the large model. These datasets typically include a mixture of copyrighted works, works in the public domain, and works eligible for fair use.

Due to the massiveness of training data, ambiguity of data sources, and technical labeling requirements, fine-grained labeling is rarely conducted. As a result, the dataset becomes a grey mixture of copyright statuses, where copyrighted works, public domain works, and fair use works are intertwined without clear boundaries, further triggering copyright infringement disputes.

Moreover, during generative AI training, the original content of the dataset is not retained; instead, the model extracts underlying patterns and stores them as discrete tokens. In this process, the characteristics of individual works become indistinct. On the output side, the algorithm extracts features from the "fed" data but also "randomly" modifies some of these features to generate new expressions. From an algorithmic perspective, it is difficult to evaluate which features of the final output of generative AI originate from which specific data in the training dataset.[3]

(3) Opacity

Large model training is characterized by technical opacity. A prominent issue in the current development of generative AI language models is the lack of transparency. Large model training is conducted in a closed environment: AI developers usually treat internal algorithm mechanisms, training processes, training data, model algorithms, parameters, and weight distributions as trade secrets to maintain competitive advantages in the field. This renders the algorithm operation process a "black box", undermining the traceability of data sources and usage. Consequently,

[3] Ye [1], p. 34.

it is impossible to confirm whether large models have used unauthorized copyrighted works, making infringement tracing and liability determination extremely difficult. Meanwhile, regulatory authorities also face significant challenges in conducting supervision and control.

From the perspective of data acquisition, model developers do not disclose the works used for training, making it hard to prove that they have used the works claimed by rights holders as training data. AI companies may employ web crawling technologies to covertly and indiscriminately collect publicly available data, or even illegally obtain grey-area data. The entire process of data acquisition and usage lacks proper documentation, resulting in untraceable data origins. Even if partial traces are left during data acquisition, the "algorithm shadow" phenomenon of training data exacerbates the difficulty of traceability. This is because even if the original training data is deleted, the features previously learned by the model have been internalized and stored as model parameters, allowing the model to still generate infringing content based on these parameters.

Furthermore, the high costs of traditional licensing models force some generative AI developers to illegally obtain training data. Taking advantage of the opacity of large model training, they use unauthorized works to avoid high expenses. Such behavior not only seriously infringes on the legitimate rights and interests of copyright holders but also disrupts the compliance order of the industry.

From the perspective of the training process, data is not directly copied during training; instead, it is "digested and absorbed" into model parameters. The model then generates new content expressions that are distinct from existing works in unpredictable ways. The content generated by generative AI is "familiar yet different" from the original works.[4] When infringement occurs, rights holders find it difficult to identify direct and obvious infringement points in the model's algorithm structure. Copyright holders can only infer infringement based on the output content. However, the output of large models is generated according to user prompts after processing data through pre-defined algorithms. Meanwhile, to avoid "overfitting" or content regurgitation, generative AI developers add rule-based program modules on the output side, combined with decoding layer constraints and post-processing verification mechanisms, further reducing the similarity between AI-generated content and original works. This makes it even harder to determine whether substantial similarity exists.

For example, in the case of Kadrey v. Meta, Meta conducted post-training on its models to prevent them from "memorizing" and outputting specific text. Even with suggestive prompts, the models could not generate content exceeding fifty words and punctuation marks. Consequently, the court ruled that no infringement had occurred.

[4] Linghan et al. [2], p. 11.

2.2 Copyright Infringement Risk Analysis of Training Data Usage

Generative AI training relies on massive volumes of high-quality data, which constitutes the foundation and core of its technological innovation. However, using such a vast array of works for model training without explicit authorization will give rise to copyright infringement risks. How to determine whether the use of generative AI training data constitutes copyright infringement, and balance the development of the generative AI industry, copyright protection, and public interests, has become an urgent issue to be resolved. This section will systematically analyze the key points of controversy in this process based on the core rights under copyright law.

2.2.1 *Infringement Determination of "Reproduction Behavior"*

Copyright is an exclusive right that controls the use of the expressive content of works, rather than all acts of using works. Only "acts of use under the meaning of copyright law" fall within the scope of copyright control and risk being deemed infringing acts. To characterize the use of generative AI, the key is to determine whether the act of use falls within the scope of exclusive copyright rights—that is, whether it constitutes an "act of use under the meaning of copyright law".[5]

The right of reproduction is the core right in the copyright system. It is an exclusive right granted by law to copyright holders to control their works, protect their economic interests in the dissemination of works, and incentivize creators to produce works. Reproduction refers to copying the content of texts, images, data, etc., to create duplicates identical to the original work. Its essence lies in the reproduction of the original work; this process does not add any original content and is merely a duplication of the original work.

Reproduction can be divided into temporary reproduction and permanent reproduction. The former refers to the temporary, automatic caching of data in a device during information processing to achieve specific technical functions—such as media playback caching or document browsing caching—which is automatically deleted when the device is shut down or restarted. At present, there are significant disputes among countries regarding whether temporary reproduction constitutes an infringement of the right of reproduction. China's Copyright Law does not recognize temporary reproduction as falling within the scope of exclusive copyright control; thus, if only temporary reproduction occurs during training, it is not an "act of use under the meaning of copyright law" and does not risk infringing the right of reproduction. However, the United States and the European Union hold that temporary reproduction is a form of reproduction right and is regulated by copyright law.

[5] Wenyi and Dongmei [3].

Permanent reproduction refers to the relatively stable and long-term fixation of a work on a specific tangible medium, enabling it to be perceived, preserved for a long time, and reused repeatedly. This type of reproduction is regulated by the right of reproduction under China's Copyright Law. The use of such works must obtain the consent of the copyright holder; otherwise, it may constitute an infringement of the right of reproduction. As defined, the core elements of permanent reproduction (hereinafter referred to as reproduction) are permanence and perceptibility. Permanence means that the work can be fixed on a tangible carrier and reused repeatedly; perceptibility means that the reproduced work can be perceived by humans directly or with the assistance of machinery or devices.

In the context of generative AI, the way large models use works for training differs from traditional reproduction. Model training involves inputting works into the model and converting them into model parameters. Whether this act constitutes an infringement of the right of reproduction should be determined by the core elements of reproduction—permanence and perceptibility. Currently, there is no unified global standard for whether inputting works into a model and converting them into parameters constitutes "reproduction".

When studying whether copyright infringement exists in generative AI data training, it is first necessary to clarify the relationship between works, training data, and training datasets. Training data is the digital carrier of works and their external form of expression, while a training dataset is a collection of training data. When works are collected in the form of training data and incorporated into a dataset, the works are in fact reproduced in digital form.[6] In other words, training data is knowledge and information expressed in a computer-readable form, which may include works protected by copyright (i.e., individual works or compiled works in the dataset). The act of digitally processing works—including converting original works into data-format duplicates or crawling already digitized works—and collectively inputting them into an intelligent system constitutes reproduction.[7]

When the Copyright Law was revised in 2020, digital reproduction was incorporated into the scope of protection of the right of reproduction. Digital reproduction mainly includes two forms: (1) reproduction from a tangible carrier to a digital carrier, i.e., converting works originally recorded on a tangible carrier into a digital format through digital scanning or similar means; (2) direct reproduction between digital carriers, i.e., copying digital works between different servers or computers through uploading, downloading, etc.[8] Therefore, the unauthorized use of rights holders' works in digital form falls within the scope of copyright holders' rights and risks infringing the right of reproduction. This infringement risk can be further analyzed by combining the training phases of generative AI.

[6] See Limei et al. [4], p. 29.

[7] Handong [5], p. 656.

[8] Handong [6].

Generative AI training is mainly divided into three phases: training data collection and processing phase, training phase, and output phase. Training Data Collection and Processing Phase.

(1) Training Data Collection and Processing Phase

During this phase, model developers typically obtain works from public websites, databases, and other channels through web crawling, convert them into training data in a format readable by large models, form a dataset, and store it on a server for subsequent model training. In this phase, developers inevitably copy and store digital duplicates of works, stably and permanently storing the works on the server—which satisfies the permanence characteristic of reproduction. Moreover, the digital duplicates can be restored after decoding, meeting the requirement of perceptibility. The unauthorized acquisition of others' copyrighted works during this phase constitutes the digital reproduction of works as stipulated in Article 12 of the Copyright Law, falls within the exclusive scope of the right of reproduction, and infringes the copyright holder's right of reproduction.

(2) Training Phase

In this phase, the model disassembles the training data in the dataset formed during the collection and processing phase into discrete token sequences, converts them into computable vectors, performs "feature extraction" on them, and finally transforms the extracted internal patterns into parameter weights to quantify the connection strength between different features. The digital duplicates in this phase are not complete work content but discrete parameters, which cannot restore the original work even after decoding. Thus, there is no unified standard for whether converting work data into parameter weights constitutes "reproduction" in this phase.

From a technical perspective, there are two model training methods:

The first method involves loading works into the temporary cache of a computer's memory or hard disk for real-time training of the large model, with data cleared immediately after training is completed. This training mode constitutes temporary reproduction, which does not fall within the scope of China's copyright regulation and thus does not constitute infringement.

The second method involves storing the model as weight parameters on a hard disk or in the cloud after training is completed. This storage method allows permanent preservation and repeated use, satisfying the permanence requirement of reproduction behavior.

A large model mainly consists of two parts: algorithms and model parameters. The core logic of algorithms is relatively stable, while model parameters are continuously adjusted during training. The adjustment logic of model parameters involves converting works such as text and images into machine-readable formats, then transforming them through algorithms to be stored in the model in digital form—which constitutes a form of "reproduction" of the work content. Although the carrier and format of the work have undergone fundamental changes, the core expressive content of the work is fixed in a new form and used for subsequent generation, which touches upon the permanence of reproduction.

In addition, machine learning is not achieved overnight. For generative AI large models, repeated training is required to improve the probability of predicting the next token. Through multiple rounds of iterative training, parameter weights are continuously adjusted to make the model's output content more accurate and in line with user needs. During multiple rounds of iterative training, the model needs to repeatedly call training data stored on a hard disk or in the cloud. This technical fact provides key evidence for determining that the model training act constitutes "permanent reproduction" of the original work in legal terms.

For perceptibility, it cannot be determined in the same way as traditional perceptibility, since parameters cannot be directly read and must be analyzed with the assistance of certain technical functions. Perceptibility can be divided into three categories:

Direct perceptibility: Refers to reproductions that can be directly perceived by humans. In the model training phase of generative AI, training data exists as discrete tokens and thus does not satisfy direct perceptibility.

Indirect perceptibility: Refers to the model's ability to stably reproduce the original work's expressive content by inputting prompts. In this case, the model parameters are essentially a memory storage carrier of the work; indirect reproduction of the original work is achieved at the output end through simple prompts, meeting the requirement of indirect perceptibility. For example, in GEMA v. OpenAI (first instance in 2025, no final judgment yet), the court ruled that OpenAI constituted infringement in both the model training and content generation phases. The court held that lyrics were fixed in digital form inside the model; even if the data was stored dispersedly, it still constituted a "fixed" duplicate. Although the parameters inside the model could not be directly extracted, the expressive content of the lyrics could be reproduced through simple prompts, which constitutes indirect perception and thus infringes the right of reproduction.

Non-perceptibility: Refers to parameters that only extract the "general features" of works—such as extracting grammatical patterns from tens of thousands of news reports without being able to reproduce any single news report. In this case, the parameters do not reproduce the expressive content of specific works, meaning they do not satisfy the requirement of perceptibility.

(3) Output Phase

The determination of whether infringement occurs in this phase adopts the "access + substantial similarity" standard. Unlike traditional access methods, in the AI era, works exist in cyberspace in virtual digital form. Human readers' access to works has shifted from copies on tangible carriers to copies in data form.[9] In this state, AI developers can more easily access and use works without leaving traces, thus increasing the difficulty of adducing evidence in infringement determination. A comprehensive determination can be made based on the substantial similarity of

[9] Handong [6].

content at the output end. When the content at the output end is highly similar to the core expression of the copyrighted work, infringement can be presumed.

However, due to the enormous volume of generative AI training data, the probability of fragments of a single work appearing in the output results is extremely low. The expression of each work usually appears in the form of small fragments. As long as the scale of training data is sufficiently large, the output content often constitutes an entirely new work. Only when the training data is extremely limited or the algorithm malfunctions may the output content replicate all or part of the original work; under normal circumstances, there is no possibility of infringing the right of reproduction.

It should be clarified, however, that the output end of generative AI is premised on the input end, and the output end is the sole effect of the input end. Infringement in the output phase is a legacy issue from the input phase, merely manifested in the output phase.[10] In other words, if the content at the output end is substantially similar to the copyrighted work, it means the large model has accessed and illegally "reproduced" the copyrighted work. This has been reflected in judicial practice—for example, in The New York Times v. OpenAI and JDoe et al. v. GitHub, highly similar works to copyrighted content can be generated through prompts, and this high similarity confirms that AI developers illegally copied copyrighted works when training their models. Additionally, in The New York Times v. OpenAI, the defendant OpenAI stated in a declaration: "Regurgitating or highlighting entire sections of specific content or articles is a rare error, and we are working to reduce it to zero." On the surface, this is a defense by the defendant, but it is equivalent to an admission that AI developers used copyrighted works when training large models, in fact constituting an infringement of the right of reproduction.

From the perspective of extraterritorial legislation, countries have established different paths for restricting exclusive copyright rights—such as the Text and Data Mining (TDM) exception clauses in the EU, the non-enjoyment use clause in Japan, and the fair use system centered on the four-factor standard in the United States. Although their names and constituent elements vary, their essence is provisions on copyright infringement exemption. The logical premise for applying these infringement exemption provisions is that the actor's conduct falls within the scope of copyright regulation and may constitute copyright infringement.

Take the EU's Copyright in the Digital Single Market Directive (DSM Directive) as an example: Articles 3 (for scientific research purposes) and 4 (for general purposes) set out TDM exceptions, allowing the reproduction, extraction, and storage of lawfully accessible works and databases. From these provisions, it can be seen that the EU recognizes to a certain extent that generative AI may risk infringing the right of reproduction when using data to train models; otherwise, it would not have specially established TDM exception clauses. Similarly, Japan's non-appreciative use clause has the same effect: both regulate the use of data by generative AI as exceptions to the right of reproduction. These provisions also imply the premise that

[10] Wenyi and Dongmei [3], p. 94.

the use of work data by generative AI during training falls within the scope of control of the right of reproduction in principle, but is included in the scope of infringement exemption based on considerations such as promoting AI technological innovation and development, and balancing public interests with the individual interests of right holders—thus restricting the exclusive rights of copyright holders. In summary, it can be inferred from EU and Japanese legislation that the acts of copying, storing, and using existing work data during generative AI training risk infringing the right of reproduction.

Copyright infringement cases occur frequently in the United States. The determination logic of the "transformative use" standard adopted by U.S. courts to determine fair use confirms, from another perspective, that AI training acts carry the risk of infringing the right of reproduction. U.S. courts' analysis of "transformative use" is usually premised on the fact that "the act of use falls within the scope of copyright regulation". Transformative use refers to the use of copyrighted works by changing the original work's form, content, function, or purpose to create derivative results with new expressions, meanings, or values—rather than merely copying or repeating the core value of the original work. Its core judgment standard is whether the act of use endows the original work with a "new purpose" or "new expression", rather than only utilizing the existing value of the original work.

For example, in the case of 13 Authors v. Meta, the court held that Meta's copying of books was not for the purpose of allowing users to read them, but to extract linguistic statistical patterns to create a tool capable of multiple functions such as email writing and programming assistance— which is completely different from the original purpose of books, i.e., providing entertainment or education through reading—and thus constitutes highly transformative use. Although the alleged act in this case was deemed transformative use and thus fair use, it also means that reproduction behavior existed during large model training, which constitutes an infringement of the right of reproduction.

In addition, some judges cite the "intermediate copying" principle established by the U.S. Court of Appeals for the Ninth Circuit in Sega v. Accolade and Sony v. Connectix. The so-called "intermediate copying" refers to the act of copying others' copyrighted works during the data training phase of generative AI models, where such copying is an intermediate step for generating new works at the output end, and the content at the output end is "transformative", which can constitute fair use under copyright law and does not amount to infringement. For example, in Thomson v. Ross, the U.S. court tended to hold that copying and using copyrighted works for training generative AI models constitutes fair use, relying on the "intermediate copying" standard. In summary, U.S. judicial practice clearly reveals a line of reasoning: although the act of using copyrighted works is exempted due to being deemed "transformative use", its starting point lies in acknowledging that the "reproduction" of copyrighted works during training has already violated the right of reproduction.

2.2.2 The Applicable Boundaries of "Fair Use": Can it Exempt Infringement Liability?

The development of generative AI technology relies on stable, high-quality, and massive copyrighted works. However, the massive scale of such works conflicts with the traditional one-to-one licensing model. Training high-performance generative AI systems inevitably requires high-quality training data—i.e., copyrighted texts, images, audio, etc.—thus carrying the risk of copyright infringement.

If we merely rely on the provisions of the Copyright Law and related regulations, while protecting the interests of copyright holders, it will hinder the development of the artificial intelligence industry and be detrimental to public interests, which is contrary to China's current national strategy of promoting AI technology development. Conversely, if generative AI developers are allowed to use copyrighted works on a large scale without permission, copyright holders will not only fail to obtain benefits from it, but also face the danger of being gradually replaced by AI-generated content.[11] Therefore, it is urgent to establish a balanced system that takes into account both the protection of copyright holders' rights and the development of AI technology, so as to achieve a win-win situation for the development of the artificial intelligence industry and the creation of works. To promote technological development and enable generative AI developers to use works for model training, incorporating data training behavior into the fair use system is an optional path.

At present, copyright infringement cases involving generative AI occur frequently around the world, and AI companies generally defend themselves by claiming that their use of training data constitutes fair use—such as in The New York Times v. OpenAI and GEMA v. OpenAI. However, due to fundamental differences in the standards for determining fair use among countries, coupled with the exercise of judges' discretionary power, similar behaviors often face completely opposite judicial outcomes in different jurisdictions. This divergence has already been reflected in historical cases. For example, in 2004, Google scanned entire works and stored them in its database for readers to search without the permission of copyright holders, triggering infringement lawsuits against Google by relevant authors in China and the United States. Courts in China and the United States reached completely opposite conclusions: Chinese courts ruled the act constituted infringement, while U.S. courts held it was fair use. The drastically different judicial treatment of the same act in China and the United States stems from the differences in fair use determination standards under different legal systems and the exercise of judges' discretionary power. In the context of generative AI, similar legal divergences have emerged again, and the issue has become more prominent and intractable due to the massiveness, hybridity, and opacity of training data.

[11] See Sag [7], p. 301.

The U.S. Fair Use System: Taking Transformative Use as the Core Standard

The United States has demonstrated its unique institutional advantages in addressing this issue. Although it has not enacted special legislation on the fair use of AI training data, its existing laws can address the copyright infringement issues of training data. Moreover, the U.S. Copyright Office pointed out in Copyright and Artificial Intelligence Part 2: Copyrightability that no special legislation is needed at present, and copyright law is sufficient to resolve the legality issues of training data. This is because Sect. 107 of the U.S. Copyright Act stipulates the four-factor test for determining fair use, namely:

The purpose and character of the use, including whether such use is of a commercial nature or is for nonprofit educational purposes;
The nature of the copyrighted work;
The amount and substantiality of the portion used in relation to the copyrighted work as a whole;
The effect of the use upon the potential market for or value of the copyrighted work.

The first factor—the purpose and character of the use—introduced the transformative use standard as the core criterion for determining fair use in the U.S. Supreme Court's Campbell v. Acuff-Rose Music, Inc. case. Transformative use refers to the use of the original work in a different manner or for a different purpose during the creation of a new work, endowing the work with creativity and new value. The degree of transformativeness is proportional to the possibility of being deemed fair use: the higher the degree of transformativeness of the secondary use, the more likely it is to be recognized as fair use.[12]

U.S. courts have applied the four-factor fair use test in multiple cases where copyright holders sued generative AI companies for unauthorized training using their works. In these cases, U.S. courts tend to rule that AI training behavior constitutes transformative use, and thus fair use, not amounting to copyright infringement. For example:

In Multiple Authors v. Anthropic, the court divided Anthropic's copying behavior into three categories—training copies, purchased and digitized library copies, and pirated library copies—and analyzed them separately. For training copies, the judge held that Anthropic copied works to train the Claude model to learn linguistic statistical patterns and create brand-new content, which is typically transformative. It did not output infringing content nor cause substitutive harm to the market of the original works, thus constituting fair use. For purchased and digitized library copies, the court ruled that this constituted format conversion; since Anthropic had paid for the works, digitized them for internal storage and search, and destroyed the paper originals, it did not infringe the authors' rights and constituted fair use. However, pirated library copies were deemed "irreparably infringing".

[12] Dezhong and Yunwei [8], p. 82.

In Thirteen Authors v. Meta, the court held that Meta's use of copyrighted books to train its AI model constituted highly transformative fair use. Meta copied the books not to allow users to read them, but to extract linguistic statistical patterns to create a tool capable of multiple functions such as email writing and programming assistance—completely different from the original purpose of books, which is to provide entertainment or education through reading. Furthermore, even with suggestive prompts, the model could only generate fragments of no more than 50 words, far from constituting market substitution.

U.S. judicial practice tends to recognize AI developers' defense of fair use and has gradually established the fair use boundary for generative AI training data centered on the "transformative use" theory. However, the U.S. four-factor test has inherent flaws: although the fair use principle is flexible, its application is not absolute and is subject to uncertainty. As an open-ended standard, the four-factor test requires balancing in individual cases, and no single factor is decisive. For example, in Thomson v. Ross, the court reached the opposite conclusion, ruling that Ross's use of Westlaw's "legal compilation annotations" to train an AI legal search tool did not constitute fair use. The reason was that both Ross and Westlaw ultimately aimed to provide legal search tools; Ross's use was commercial in nature and directly created market substitutes with highly overlapping product functions.

At present, these major landmark cases are still pending. Before the federal appellate courts or the Supreme Court issue binding final judgments, there is no final conclusion on the scope of application and judgment standards of the "fair use" principle, and its specific boundaries remain to be further clarified. Therefore, neither party can obtain a final determination of its legal status at this stage.

China's Fair Use System: A Relatively Closed Regime with Limited Exemption Space

In China, fair use refers to the use of a copyright holder's published work by a user without permission and without payment of remuneration under statutory circumstances, provided that the name of the author or the title of the work is indicated, the normal use of the work is not affected, and the legitimate rights and interests of the copyright holder are not unreasonably prejudiced.[13] At present, regarding the legal nature of copyright fair use in China, the infringement obstruction theory occupies a mainstream position in the academic circle of law. This theory holds that fair use is essentially a ground for obstructing copyright infringement. Specifically, unauthorized use of others' works constitutes copyright infringement under normal circumstances, but if it meets the statutory conditions for fair use, the act may not be deemed infringing. This is a copyright exemption mechanism that exempts acts that would otherwise constitute copyright infringement under certain conditions.

[13] Article 24(1), Copyright Law of the People's Republic of China.

Incorporating the act of generative AI using training data into the scope of fair use has certain merits. Under the traditional licensing model, AI developers must pay high costs to obtain training data; otherwise, the lack of massive data will affect the objectivity and accuracy of large models, leading to bias, homogenization, and low quality. Adopting the fair use system can reduce the cost for enterprises to obtain author authorization, ensure that training data meets the quantity, error, and completeness requirements for large model training, and guarantee that large models are aligned with human values.[14]

Compared with the U.S. four-factor test for determining fair use, China's fair use rules are relatively closed, making it difficult to determine exemption from reproduction right infringement, and the exemption space provided for AI training is extremely limited. At present, China's judicial practice mainly adopts the three-step test derived from the Berne Convention as the standard for determining whether an actor's conduct constitutes fair use:

The use must be limited to the statutory circumstances specified in Article 24 of the Copyright Law;
The use must not affect the normal use of the work;
The use must not unreasonably prejudice the legitimate rights and interests of the copyright holder.

The three-step test adopts a progressive determination method, where the latter two steps grant judges discretionary power within the scope of statutory types, which needs to be comprehensively judged in combination with specific cases. At present, the "three-step test" faces interpretive difficulties in determining whether the act of generative AI using training data can apply the fair use system.

(1) Obstacles to Satisfying the First Step: Compliance with Statutory Circumstances.

The primary requirement is that the use must conform to statutory circumstances. In the scenario of generative AI training, there are significant obstacles to the judicial determination of this standard. Among the statutory circumstances stipulated in the Copyright Law, the relevant circumstances applicable to the exemption from infringement of generative AI training data mainly include personal use, appropriate quotation, scientific research, and the catch-all clause. However, a closer examination reveals difficulties in application:

Personal use clause: Due to the requirements of this clause regarding the subject and purpose of use, generative AI data training does not meet the conditions for application. First, the subject of use is limited to natural persons, while the subject using works in generative AI training is AI developers. Although specific natural persons train large models, this act is part of performing their job duties, and the ultimate subject of use should be deemed as the AI developer, usually a legal person. Second, this clause requires the purpose of use to be study, research, or

[14] Jiangang [9], p. 69.

appreciation, while AI developers use digitized works to facilitate large model learning, but their ultimate purpose is commercial use to obtain economic benefits.

Appropriate quotation clause: Its requirements for the quantity and purpose of using works are inconsistent with the characteristics of generative AI. The requirement of "appropriate quantity" in this clause contradicts the technical characteristic of large models using massive data for training, and the purpose of large models using works is not to "introduce, comment on a work or explain a problem".

Scientific research clause: It cannot be applied due to inconsistencies in the purpose and quantity of use. On the one hand, the purpose of use requires the user to use the work for classroom teaching or scientific research, which is non-profit in nature, while training generative AI is for profit even if it is related to scientific research. On the other hand, the use for scientific research requires a "small amount", including both the "small amount" of the total quantity of works used and the "small amount" of the proportion of the used part in a single work,[15] which contradicts the technical characteristic of generative AI data training requiring massive data.

Catch-all clause: There are currently no provisions in laws or administrative regulations on whether it can be used to determine the act of generative AI data training, and further provisions are needed to clarify this point.

In summary, there are obstacles to the application of all statutory circumstances for fair use, which will make it difficult to apply the three-step test for exemption from infringement.

(2) Difficulties in Satisfying the Latter Two Steps: No Impact on Normal Use and No Prejudice to Legitimate Rights and Interests.

Even if the catch-all clause applicable to the fair use system can be invoked at present, it is difficult to meet the latter two standards—i.e., the requirement that the use does not affect the normal use of the work and does not prejudice the legitimate rights and interests of the copyright holder. China's institutional transplantation of the Berne Convention's "three-step test" only stays at the level of borrowing legislative provisions rather than interpretive rules. In judicial practice, conclusions from judge-made law in common law countries are even directly introduced to resolve relevant cases, leading to the loss of predictability and operability of the judicial determination standards for fair use.[16] In the era of generative AI, the judgment of "normal use" and "prejudice to legitimate rights and interests" will become more complex.

On the one hand, AI developers generally claim that their use of training data is to learn the style of works, not the original expression. Even if this claim is true, when AI can highly imitate and generate works of a certain style on a large scale, it will inevitably impact the market of the original works, constituting an impact on the "normal use of the copyrighted work" and prejudice to the "legitimate interests

[15] Lili [10], p. 162.

[16] Qi [11], p. 182.

of the copyright holder".[17] On the other hand, the complex relationship between the model's output content and the original work makes it difficult to accurately assess whether the legitimate rights and interests of the copyright holder are prejudiced. The training process of generative AI often involves the use of a large number of unauthorized copyrighted works, and the way these works are used is relatively vague, making it difficult to judge whether they will cause unreasonable prejudice to the rights and interests of the original copyright holders, as well as whether they will have a far-reaching impact on the market demand and dissemination methods of the original works.

(3) Conflict with the Purpose of the Fair Use System.

The purpose of the fair use system is to balance the personal interests of copyright holders and social public interests. By allowing potential users to freely use works without payment, it ensures that the public can access knowledge and enhance the well-being of the whole people. At the same time, it requires that the incentive for copyright holders will not be substantially damaged by allowing users to continue using the works [[57]], thereby solving market failure problems and improving overall social efficiency. However, the development of generative AI technology must rely on massive, high-quality data, which inevitably requires the use of copyrighted works. There is a tension between allowing developers to use works for free and requiring right holders to pay for related AI uses. The lack of protection for copyright holders will dampen their enthusiasm for creation, leading to a reduction in works full of human touch. Generative AI will lose its "nutrients", and what circulates widely in society will be machine-generated works lacking individual perception, emotion, and experience, ultimately harming social public interests.[18]

Conclusion: Low Possibility of Exemption from Liability under China's Current Legal Framework

Under China's current legal framework, the boundaries of the fair use system are relatively clear and narrow. However, whether generative AI training can fall within its scope has neither explicit legal provisions nor the support of judicial precedents. Therefore, the possibility of claiming fair use to exempt infringement liability for relevant acts is low, and the risk is high.

It is worth noting that although some related cases have been concluded, none of them have made judgments on the core legal issue of whether training behavior constitutes fair use. For example, in the 2024 "Ultraman" case, the defendant's website used artificial intelligence to generate images substantially similar to the copyrighted "Ultraman" images owned by the plaintiff without authorization. The court ultimately supported the plaintiff's main claims, ruled that the defendant constituted

[17] Yifan [12], p. 185.

[18] Mingxuan [13], p. 33.

infringement, and required it to fulfill the "duty of care" and "duty of identification" to avoid generating copyright-infringing images. However, regarding the plaintiff's claim to delete the Ultraman copyrighted images involved in the defendant's website's generative AI training set, the court held that the defendant was only a user rather than a trainer of artificial intelligence, and thus could not enforce the deletion operation. In essence, this judgment only ruled on issues in the "generation phase" and failed to provide substantive guidance on the determination of infringement in the "training phase" and the application of the fair use system.

In addition, although the Hangzhou Internet Court did not make a clear ruling on the act of generative AI training using data in the Ultraman infringement case, the judgment indicated a future trend: "A prudent and inclusive attitude should be adopted towards generative AI to encourage technological progress and commercial development. The creation and development of generative AI require massive training data, which inevitably involves the use of others' works. This kind of use aggregates a large number of works as analysis sample data for training to improve work creation capabilities, not for the purpose of reproducing the original expression of the works. In general, data training only temporarily retains prior works when conducting structural feature analysis of corpus data, and neither the data training nor the generation process displays the prior works to the public. Therefore, in the absence of evidence proving that the purpose of generative AI is to use the original expression of the copyrighted work, that it has affected the normal use of the copyrighted work, or that it has unreasonably prejudiced the legitimate interests of the relevant copyright holders, such use can be deemed as fair use."[19]

2.2.3 *Defensive Space for Statutory License and "Implied License"*

In addition to fair use, copyright law also provides for statutory license as a restriction on the exclusive rights of copyright holders. Statutory license allows users to use copyrighted works that have been published without the copyright holder's consent under statutory circumstances, but requires payment of remuneration to the copyright holder. As an intermediate system between the protection of authors' exclusive rights and the fair use system established for public interests, statutory license not only has the advantage of fair use in reducing authorization difficulties, but also can protect the legitimate interests of copyright holders to a certain extent—that is, users must pay remuneration to copyright holders in accordance with regulations.

However, under China's current closed legislative model, there are obstacles to applying statutory license to generative AI training data for infringement exemption:

[19] Shanghai XX Cultural Development Co., Ltd. v. Hangzhou XX Intelligent Technology Co., Ltd. (Copyright Infringement and Unfair Competition Case), (2024) Zhe 0192 Min Chu No. 1587.

Restricted to specific statutory circumstances: Current copyright legislation in China only stipulates five types of statutory licenses—compiling textbooks, reprinting by newspapers and periodicals, producing sound recordings, broadcasting works, and creating courseware—as well as a quasi-statutory license: providing specific works to rural areas through the internet. Generative AI training data cannot be categorized into any of these circumstances.

High cost and pricing difficulties: Generative AI training requires massive works, which means high statutory license fees must be paid. Moreover, the pricing of statutory licenses is difficult to adapt to the flexible and variable market. Statutory license weakens the exclusivity of property rights mainly through the transfer of pricing power. However, whether the pricing power is negotiated through representative negotiations and then approved by the copyright competent authority, or directly determined by the copyright competent authority, it is difficult to overcome the inherent defects of the statutory price mechanism.[20] In addition, the contribution of a single dataset to the model as a whole varies in different training stages, leading to pricing difficulties. The learning stage is mainly divided into pre-training and fine-tuning: pre-training uses a large amount of unlabeled text data to train the model to learn language representations and patterns; in this stage, massive data is used, and the role of a single dataset is not prominent. As the number of parameters increases, the impact of a single dataset on the model decreases. Fine-tuning is the further training of the pre-trained model to adapt to specific tasks, improve model performance, and enhance its generalization ability. This stage requires high-quality data, and the quality of data has a great impact on the model. For all datasets used in the pre-training and fine-tuning stages, it is difficult to quantify the contribution of each dataset to the model, making it impossible to evaluate the value and price of a single dataset.

As mentioned above, neither fair use nor statutory license can fully address the issue of infringement exemption for AI training data usage. Implied license, however, may provide an alternative legal solution for AI. Unlike statutory license, implied license infers the copyright holder's permission for the user to use the work from the holder's conduct or silence under specific circumstances; it is a presumed voluntary license, but reserves the right of opt-out for the copyright holder.

Model developers mainly use data for model training based on the terms of content platforms signed with right holders. Taking GitHub as an example, Section D.4 of its Terms of Service stipulates that right holders grant the platform the right to store, archive, parse, display your content, and make incidental copies, but only to the extent necessary to provide the service, including improving the service over time. Although this clause does not directly mention "allowing AI training use", GitHub actually defines the act of training its AI model using massive public code repositories as part of improving GitHub products or services. Therefore, when a right holder registers a GitHub account and uploads a work, they have implicitly accepted the platform's Terms of Service—that is, the platform can use the work for

[20] Xinming and Ye [14].

training AI large models. In principle, therefore, the right holder's use of the platform constitutes permission for the platform to use the content for AI large model training. However, based on respect for developers' wishes and community pressure, GitHub proposed a code repository exclusion mechanism in its official policy statement for Copilot, its AI large model—that is, users have the right to opt out of their works being used for AI large model training. At present, AI trainers generally adopt similar strategies: their User Agreements or Terms of Service generally include broad authorization clauses for using user content "to improve services and develop new products". When users check the consent box and upload content, they are deemed to have implicitly licensed the platform to use the user-published works for AI large model training through their conduct. The implied license system solves the efficiency and cost problems of massive authorization to a certain extent, while fully considering the copyright holder's authorization intention by endowing them with the right to opt out. If the copyright holder refuses, the user will not obtain authorization. In addition, it is conducive to the utilization of works, encourages innovation, promotes the development of the artificial intelligence industry, and conforms to public interests.

Nevertheless, there are practical difficulties in application:

Legal uncertainty of standard terms: Provisions represented by GitHub's Terms of Service are essentially standard terms, which have legal uncertainty. The true purpose of such clauses is often hidden in complex textual expressions; they are formulated unilaterally by the platform without communication or negotiation with right holders. The agreement reached on this basis may be deemed invalid standard terms.

Negative impact of the "opt-out" right on technological development: The actual operation of the "opt-out" right may lead to results that are contrary to the needs of technological development. If users are allowed to use "implied license" as a defense, in theory, all copyright holders have the right to opt out. To protect their own interests, a widespread opt-out may occur. For generative AI, training data is like the "nutrient" for technological development. Once a large number of works cannot be used due to right holders' opt-out, the scale and quality of training datasets will drop significantly, directly leading to the dilemma of AI model training being "unable to cook without rice", and ultimately hindering the development of artificial intelligence technology.

Misapplication of implied license in web crawling scenarios: When third parties obtain publicly available works through web crawling technology for model training, since there is no agreement such as service terms with copyright holders, claiming implied license only on the grounds that the works are publicly accessible violates the essential requirements of implied license. The premise of implied license is that there is a certain legal relationship or consensus basis between the two parties, such as the service agreement between the platform and the user. However, publicly available works obtained through web crawling technology are often content publicly disseminated by right holders on the internet; such public availability only means that the works can be accessed by the public, and does not equate to implied authorization for AI training use. There is neither a written agreement such as service terms nor any actual communication between the third party and the copyright holder. Claiming implied license only on the grounds that "the work is publicly accessible" is essentially a confusion of the concepts of "publicity" and "authorization", which constitutes improper use of copyright and seriously infringes on the legitimate rights and interests of the right holder.

In summary, although the fair use, statutory license, and implied license systems have theoretical legitimacy for copyright infringement defense, all three face practical application difficulties. The dispute over the legality of generative AI data training involves personal interests, property interests, and social public interests. The conflicts and games between different interests reflect the tension between "strict copyright protection" and "free use of works", and the balance between "private interests" and "public interests".[21] Taking scientific research institutions using AI to analyze ancient books and documents as an example, although it is commercial in nature, the social benefits it brings are far higher than personal interests. AI's super learning ability can efficiently and systematically tap the historical and cultural value contained in ancient books and documents, break through the efficiency and scope bottlenecks of manual research, promote the popularization and dissemination of ancient book knowledge, bring traditional culture into the public eye, and realize the inheritance and protection of ancient books and documents. In this case, it is more legitimate for scientific research institutions to use AI to analyze ancient books and documents, and they can claim public interest as a defense. However, for using AI to analyze general copyrighted works, the social value brought is lower than that of ancient books and documents, and the possibility of defending on the grounds of public interest is slim, so other paths for exemption need to be explored.

In conclusion, the infringement exemption for the legality of training data requires a comprehensive balance of the interests of relevant stakeholders. From the perspective of copyright protection, massive high-quality training data is the "nutrient" for AI technology development. Determining that generative AI's use of unauthorized works for data training constitutes copyright infringement will cause a source-level obstacle to AI technological innovation, cut off the path of knowledge dissemination using AI technology, and thus harm social public interests. From the perspective of promoting AI technology development, allowing the unauthorized use of copyrighted works will damage the economic interests of copyright holders, reduce their enthusiasm for creation, and affect the development of the entire creative industry in the long run. Therefore, it is necessary to further clarify the conflicts of interest among all parties in the process of using copyrighted works by generative AI, reasonably balance the interests of all parties, and explore a system that not only meets the needs of the country's AI development strategy, but also protects the legitimate interests of copyright holders.

[21] Xinming and Ye [14], p. 30.

2.3 Global Regulatory Practices and Trends for Training Data Copyright Compliance

Global copyright compliance governance for generative AI training data presents a pattern of regional path differentiation, regulatory-technical synergy, and strengthened transparency and traceability. The EU implements strict regulation based on the "authorization-first" principle; the U.S. adopts flexible regulation centered on fair use; China practices transitional regulation grounded in "compliance guidelines"; and Japan enforces lenient regulation under the "non-enjoyment use" framework. All countries are striving to strike the optimal balance between AI technological development and copyright protection—one that safeguards technological innovation vitality, unlocks industrial development potential, consolidates the institutional defense line for intellectual property protection, and avoids the dual dilemmas of innovation stagnation or rights abuse caused by regulatory gaps or excessive restrictions.

2.3.1 The U.S.: Flexible Regulation Centered on "Fair Use"

As a common law country, the U.S. has not explicitly adopted legislative or judicial policies that comprehensively prioritize the development of the AI industry. Instead, it has continued its responsive strategy applied to technologies such as sound recording, broadcasting, and the internet. On one hand, it conducts extensive legislative hearings to encourage industries and social sectors to fully express their institutional demands and rationales. On the other hand, it encourages copyright industry and AI industry entities to articulate their interests through litigation, using these cases to calibrate the boundaries and standards of institutional arrangements.[22] This reflects the U.S.' relatively prudent stance on copyright compliance for generative AI training data, with an overall policy orientation characterized by "light regulation, heavy development". It aims to promote AI technological innovation, unleash AI potential, maintain its global leadership in the generative AI field, and prevent premature or overly stringent regulation from hindering technological progress.

(1) Legislative Dimensions

The U.S. Congress has not enacted dedicated AI legislation. Instead, it primarily relies on the existing legal framework, supplemented by industry-development oriented policies and framework guiding principles to govern generative AI—such as the National Artificial Intelligence Initiative Act. Additionally, the U.S. Copyright Office stated in Copyright and Artificial Intelligence Part 2: Copyrightability that copyright law is sufficient to address the legality of training data, and no special legislation is needed at present. Later, it released Copyright and Artificial Intelligence

[22] Qi and Wenyao [15], p. 66.

Part 3: Generative AI Training (Prepublication Version), which focuses on applying copyright law and fair use defense to companies using copyrighted works to train AI models. It further clarifies that the first and fourth factors of the fair use test deserve priority consideration: whether the use constitutes transformative use, and whether it poses a potential threat to the potential market of the original work.

In contrast to the federal government's prudent stance, California—an AI industry hub—has shown active momentum in AI legislation. Guided by the governance philosophy of "technology first, soft law-driven", it focuses on generative AI and implements joint governance of training data and generated synthetic content through transparency requirements.[23] In 2024, California enacted and passed the Generative Artificial Intelligence Training Data Transparency Act, which sets comprehensive transparency requirements for AI training datasets. The Act applies to developers of generative AI systems or services publicly available on the market, mandating that developers publish documents on their official websites containing details such as dataset sources, ownership, intended uses, and summaries of datasets used in system development.

Beyond California, states including Alabama, Colorado, and Illinois have also adopted AI-related legislation, though their regulatory scope remains limited. For example, Illinois focuses on regulating bias in AI systems used for employment decisions; Colorado prioritizes consumer protection in interactions with AI systems; and Alabama's legislation merely establishes an AI advisory committee.

(2) Administrative Regulatory Dimensions.

Former U.S. President Trump adopted a broad stance on AI regulation, signing an executive order in January 2025 to abolish "existing policies and directives that hinder U.S. AI innovation", though the scope of application of this order has not been clearly defined. Building on this, the U.S. government released the Winning the AI Race: U.S. Artificial Intelligence Action Plan on July 23, 2025, to further advance the domestic AI industry. Focused on federal agencies, the Plan requires accelerating the deployment of U.S.-based AI tools, while reserving sufficient flexibility to adapt to various customized needs. It establishes three core goals: accelerating AI innovation, building U.S. AI infrastructure, and leading international AI diplomacy.

In addition, federal agencies including the Federal Trade Commission (FTC), the Department of Housing and Urban Development (HUD), and the Equal Employment Opportunity Commission (EEOC) also supervise AI systems, though their regulatory scope is inherently limited by their mandates. For instance, the FTC's supervision is restricted to addressing discriminatory and fraudulent commercial practices; the EEOC focuses on AI used in recruitment and workplace applications.

(3) Judicial Practice Dimensions

[23] Qihang and Leilei [16], p. 120.

In judicial practice, the U.S. primarily relies on the four-factor fair use test to determine compliance with copyright law, thereby regulating the copyright compliance of training data. It does not completely exclude the possibility of applying the fair use system to generative AI training; even commercial use can qualify as fair use if it meets the four-factor criteria.

In Multiple Authors v. Anthropic, the court ruled that Anthropic's use of training copies to train its Claude model—for the purpose of learning linguistic patterns to generate entirely new content—constituted transformative use. Since this use did not cause substitutive harm to the traditional book market, it was deemed fair use.

Conversely, in Thomson v. Ross, the court reached the opposite conclusion. It held that Ross's use of Westlaw's legal compilation annotations to train its AI model did not constitute fair use, as the use was directly commercially competitive. The AI tool developed by Ross directly replaced users' demand for Westlaw database subscriptions, harmed the potential market of the original work, and failed to achieve a high degree of transformativeness.

As a common law country, the U.S. has unique advantages: it can form preliminary regulatory rules through individual cases, and such regulation is characterized by ex post facto accountability. This approach can promptly and flexibly regulate infringement in the field of training data copyright compliance, curb continuous infringement against copyright holders, and effectively safeguard their legitimate rights and interests. At the same time, it enables dynamic responses to various new issues arising in the process of technological development, while preserving space for enterprise innovation and development. Authoritative judicial precedents issued by U.S. courts are legally binding on subsequent similar cases, meaning its regulatory rules can be gradually accumulated and evolved through rulings in numerous specific cases, inherently possessing adaptability and flexibility.

In summary, the U.S. maintains a conservative and wait-and-see attitude toward AI training data copyright issues. At the federal level, it is development-oriented, relying on existing copyright law provisions and judicial precedents to make flexible case-by-case judgments. Its fundamental goal is to reserve sufficient space for technological innovation in this emerging field where laws and regulations remain unclear, dynamically balance the legitimate rights and interests of all parties through flexible regulation, and form preliminary rules through judicial practice that evolve dynamically.

2.3.2 *EU: Strict Regulation Based on the "Authorization-First" Principle*

In contrast to the U.S. regulatory model of "light regulation, heavy development", the EU tends to emphasize rights protection and risk prevention, establishing a strict regulatory framework centered on the authorization-first principle through forward-looking legislation. The EU has adopted a comprehensive and stringent legislative strategy for AI supervision, enacting laws and regulations such as the Artificial Intelligence Act (AI Act), the Code of Practice for General-Purpose Artificial Intelligence Systems, and the Copyright in the Digital Single Market Directive (DSM Directive), thereby solidifying its strict regulatory regime based on the authorization-first principle.

1. Core Regulatory Requirements under the AI Act

Article 53 of the EU's AI Act stipulates the obligations of providers of General-Purpose Artificial Intelligence (GPAI) models. A GPAI model is defined as an AI model trained through large-scale self-supervised learning on massive datasets; regardless of its market launch method, it features significant generality, is capable of performing a wide range of diverse tasks, and can be integrated into various downstream systems or applications. This definition excludes AI models solely used for research, development, and prototyping activities prior to market release.

Against this backdrop, Article 53 imposes two key obligations on generative AI service providers regarding training data:

Respect for copyright opt-out declarations: Article 53(1)(c) mandates that GPAI model providers must respect the rights reservation declarations made in accordance with Article 4(3) of the DSM Directive. Specifically, providers are prohibited from including works explicitly opted out by copyright holders in the scope of reproduction or extraction for Text and Data Mining (TDM). If such works are to be used, explicit authorization from the copyright holder is mandatory.

Transparency and disclosure obligations for training data: Article 53(1)(d) establishes the obligation of GPAI model providers to disclose detailed summaries of their training data, with further clarifications provided in Recital 107 of the AI Act. To implement this requirement effectively, the EU has issued the Code of Practice for AI and Template for Summarizing Training Data, which elaborates on the transparency and copyright compliance requirements that GPAI model providers must adhere to. The template covers a wide range of data categories, including publicly available datasets, private datasets, crawled web content, user data, and synthetic data. Providers are required to disclose the sources and nature of the data, but are not obligated to reveal details of the specific data or works used for model training. This regulatory design aims to ensure overall transparency in the development and deployment process, as well as compliance with copyright law, rather than demanding granular precision in data disclosure.

2. Exemptions and Supplementary Provisions under the DSM Directive

While the copyright compliance and transparency obligations under Article 53 of the AI Act are rigorous, they are not absolute. Recital 25 of the EU AI Act[24] explicitly excludes AI systems and models developed and put into use for scientific

[24] European Parliament. EU Artificial Intelligence Act [EB/OL]. [2025-12-15]. https://artificialintelligenceact.eu/recital/25/.

research and development purposes from the scope of the Act; these entities may voluntarily choose whether to disclose information related to training data.

When combined with the rules of the DSM Directive, the scope of exemptions can be further clarified:

Non-profit research institutions: Purely scientific research activities conducted by non-profit entities are eligible for the copyright exception under Article 3 of the DSM Directive, meaning no remuneration needs to be paid to copyright holders.

For-profit entities: Scientific research and development activities carried out by for-profit entities fall outside the scope of Article 3 of the DSM Directive. Instead, they must comply with Article 4 of the Directive and relevant remuneration provisions, and pay reasonable compensation to copyright holders.

3. Assessment of the EU Regulatory Model

The EU's strict regulatory framework based on the "authorization-first" principle has effectively safeguarded the rights and interests of copyright holders to a certain extent. By mandating explicit authorization for the use of copyrighted works in AI training (except for exempt scenarios) and imposing mandatory transparency obligations, it has established clear boundaries for the use of training data, reducing the risk of unauthorized use of copyrighted content.

However, this overly stringent regulatory approach may also pose potential obstacles to the development of generative AI technology. The authorization-first principle requires AI developers to obtain permission from a large number of copyright holders for training data use, which will significantly increase the cost and complexity of model development—especially for small and medium-sized enterprises with limited resources. In addition, the strict transparency and disclosure obligations may also expose the technical details and core competitiveness of AI enterprises, further restricting the innovation vitality of the industry.

2.3.3 China: Transitional Regulation Based on "Compliance Guidelines"

Unlike the EU's strict "authorization-first" regulation and the U.S.' flexible "fair use"-centered oversight, China's copyright regulation of AI training data is currently in a transitional phase characterized by "clear principles but limited details". Regulatory authorities have established a basic framework for copyright compliance of generative AI training data through China-specific compliance systems—such as the Interim Measures for the Administration of Generative Artificial Intelligence Services (hereafter referred to as the Interim Measures).

As a core driver of the technological revolution and industrial transformation, AI is a strategic technology sector critical to leading scientific advancement, enhancing national competitiveness, and safeguarding national security. Although generative AI is still in its early developmental stage, its status as a core trend in future technology is undisputed. It is therefore imperative to establish an inclusive institutional environment and adopt a prudent yet accommodative regulatory stance to foster innovation in AI technology. The principle of "accommodation" requires a flexible approach to emerging formats where uncertainties outweigh certainties, creating a favorable environment for new productive forces while upholding non-negotiable safety redlines. The principle of "prudence" mandates a tolerant "observation period" for nascent industries, while strictly cracking down on intellectual property infringement and other violations.[25]

In the early stages of AI development, the core goal is to encourage innovation and growth in generative AI, providing ample room for the AI industry to thrive. Proactive, forward-looking legislation—similar to the EU's approach—would be inappropriate for regulating copyright compliance of generative AI training data. This is due to the inherent tension between the lengthy legislative cycle and the rapid evolution of AI technology. While forward-looking legislation could address copyright infringement risks, high-performance generative AI systems rely on massive volumes of high-quality copyrighted works. Misguided proactive legislation risks hindering or even stifling the development of the generative AI industry. At the same time, this phase still requires establishing rules and measures to guide AI development while safeguarding copyright holders' legitimate rights. Thus, transitional regulation guided by compliance rules—with space reserved for AI innovation—represents the most suitable approach.

(1) Core Regulatory Principles and Requirements

Principles in the Interim Measures: Article 3 of the Interim Measures emphasizes balancing development and security, integrating innovation promotion with law-based governance, and adopting effective measures to encourage generative AI innovation. It mandates a "prudent yet accommodative" and "category-specific, tiered" regulatory framework for generative AI services. Article 7 further stipulates that "training data shall not infringe on others' intellectual property rights." These provisions remain principled and lack specific standards, intentionally leaving sufficient room for the generative AI industry to grow.

Supporting Technical Guidelines: On March 1, 2024, the National Network Security Standardization Technical Committee released the Basic Security Requirements for Generative Artificial Intelligence Services, which sets out copyright-related content security requirements for generative AI service providers. Paragraph 5.2(b) specifies that providers must "focus on identifying copyright infringement in corpora containing literary, artistic, or scientific works, as well as in generated content; if infringement is identified, the provider shall not use the relevant corpus for training." While non-mandatory, this technical guideline provides valuable guidance for copyright compliance.

(2) Advantages of the Compliance-Guided Regulatory Model

[25] Da [17], p. 82.

Reserving a Development Window: Through administrative regulations and interim measures, this model provides a flexible, predictable compliance framework for generative AI, allowing enterprises to innovate without excessive regulatory constraints.

Balancing Flexibility and Deterrence: Leveraging the strong intervention capabilities of administrative authorities, the model enables timely revisions or supplements to rules in response to industry risks or misconduct. Law enforcement agencies retain significant discretion to make case-specific judgments based on factors such as AI technological progress and public interests.

Accumulating Experience for Long-Term Rulemaking: Regulators gain time to observe AI technological trajectories, technical pathways, and potential infringement patterns, laying the groundwork for more refined, contextually appropriate laws and implementation rules. Once AI technology matures and risks are fully understood, the Interim Measures can be upgraded to formal legislation, establishing a stable, long-term regulatory mechanism to ensure the steady development of the AI industry.

China's transitional, compliance-guided regulatory model aims to balance the dual goals of AI technological advancement and copyright protection. While it provides space for AI industry growth, it also faces risks of potential market misconduct. Regulators must carefully manage the pace of oversight during this transitional period—addressing emerging issues promptly, guiding AI development proactively, and facilitating the industry's maturation. The ultimate goal is to transition from compliance guidelines to institutionalized, long-term regulation.

2.3.4 *Other Regions: Differentiated Explorations*

(1) Japan: Lenient Regulation with Flexible Fair Use

Compared to Europe and the U.S., Japan has emerged as a "haven for AI training," adopting a relatively permissive stance on copyright compliance for generative AI training data. Through three rounds of amendments to its Copyright Act, Japan has established a flexible fair use system centered on Articles 30–4 and 47–5, which serve as the primary basis for determining whether AI training data use complies with copyright law.

Article 30–4 (Non-Enjoyment-Based Use): This article permits the use of works "without the purpose of appreciating the ideas or emotions expressed therein," provided such use is "within necessary limits" and does not "unfairly prejudice copyright holders' interests." It expands the scope and methods of fair use, allowing information analysis for AI training to qualify as fair use (and thus avoid infringement) if it meets necessity, legal sourcing, and non-prejudice to holders' market interests.

Article 47–5 (Incidental Public Provision): This article allows "minor incidental use" of works to provide information processing results to the public, within necessary limits. However, if the user knows the provision is infringing and the use "unfairly prejudices copyright holders' interests" (based on work type, purpose, and form), it no longer qualifies as fair use and may constitute infringement. This rule helps deter generative AI from using infringing content and urges developers to source training data legally.

To further clarify implementation, Japan's Agency for Cultural Affairs released the Opinions on AI and Copyright-Related Issues on March 15, 2024, providing official interpretations of Article 30–4. It clarifies that data training—except for "malicious training targeting specific works"—will generally qualify as fair use. On July 31, 2024, the Agency issued the Guidelines on AI and Copyright, offering practical guidance to AI trainers, service providers, and copyright holders on risk prevention and rights protection.

While Japan's expanded fair use scope and supportive guidelines create a flexible, innovation-friendly environment, this lenient approach has faced opposition from creators, who argue it may infringe their copyrights and dampen creative incentives. Japan has yet to fully resolve the balance between technological development and copyright protection, requiring further institutional refinements to achieve long-term win-win outcomes for innovation and rights safeguarding.

(2) UK: Balancing Innovation and Rights via Collective Licensing

The UK first introduced text and data mining (TDM) exceptions in its Copyright, Designs and Patents Act 1988 (Article 29A) during a 2014 amendment, but these were limited to non-commercial research purposes. In recent years, the UK government has recognized that strict, burdensome regulations would hinder AI innovation and that existing copyright rules—restricting fair use to non-commercial activities—fail to support generative AI development. It has thus proposed multiple legislative amendments to extend infringement exceptions to commercial TDM.[26]

Unsuccessful Reform Attempts: In 2022, the UK government proposed expanding TDM exceptions to commercial use, permitting TDM for commercial purposes "unless rights holders opt out." This faced fierce opposition from creative industries (e.g., music organizations, copyright associations) and academia, leading to the proposal's withdrawal. On December 17, 2024, the UK Intellectual Property Office launched another public consultation on expanding TDM exceptions—again including a rights holder opt-out mechanism—to explore balanced solutions and provide clearer rules for AI developers and rights holders. No dedicated legislation has been enacted to date.

Policy Support and Voluntary Frameworks: In 2023, the UK Department for Science, Innovation and Technology released the white paper An Innovation-Focused Approach to AI Regulation, which outlines a principles-based regulatory framework for AI. It empowers existing regulators to interpret and implement AI-related rules within their mandates, emphasizing five core principles—including

[26] Jieru and He [18].

"appropriate transparency" and "explainability"—which require enhanced transparency of training data and disclosure of data sources throughout the AI lifecycle.[27]

On January 13, 2025, the UK government launched the AI Opportunities Action Plan, aiming to unlock AI's potential through policy support, funding, and international cooperation while ensuring global AI leadership. For AI security, it proposes improving TDM systems, funding AI regulators, establishing accountability mechanisms, and implementing regulatory sandboxes to support industry growth.[28]

In May 2025, three major UK organizations—the Copyright Licensing Agency (CLA), Authors' Licensing and Collecting Society (ALCS), and Publishers' Licensing Service (PLS)—announced plans to launch a collective licensing framework for AI training. This "opt-in" framework will allow AI developers to use text-based published works (e.g., books, journals) for training, fine-tuning, and retrieval-augmented generation (RAG), while ensuring creators receive fair compensation. Scheduled for launch in Q3 2025 (following further publisher consultations), the framework will be managed by the CLA, with royalties distributed to rights holders after deducting operational costs. It will complement (not replace) direct custom licenses between large publishers/rights holders and AI companies, particularly benefiting small creators and independent publishers who lack negotiating leverage. Licensees must also comply with strict transparency requirements, including reporting works used, content acquisition methods, and downstream uses.[29]

(3) South Korea: Guidelines and Foundational AI Legislation

In 2021, South Korean legislators proposed amending the Copyright Act (modeled after Japan's legislation) to add Article 43, which would permit the reproduction and public transmission of lawfully accessed works "within necessary limits" for "generating additional information or value." This amendment aimed to promote value-added use of existing works but lapsed in May 2024 due to the expiration of the parliamentary term.

To address AI training-related copyright disputes, the Korea Copyright Commission established an "AI Copyright System Improvement Task Force" (comprising academics, legal/technical experts, and stakeholders) and released the Generative AI Copyright Guidelines in January 2024. The guidelines provide recommendations for three key parties to avoid infringement:

AI Trainers: Ensure legal data sourcing (e.g., paying royalties, using public domain works) during model training; implement filtering mechanisms to reduce similarity between generated content and copyrighted works.

Copyright Holders: Opt out of AI training via website terms of service or machine-readable notices to exclude their works from training data.

---

[27] Daoqin [19], p. 21.

[28] UK Releases AI Action Plan to Promote a Decade of National Revitalization. Cybersecurity and Informatization Trends, 2025(1). https://ecas.cas.cn/xxkw/kbcd/201115_146615/ml/xxhzlyzc/202501/t20250117_5045365.html.

[29] See UK's Collective Licensing Scheme Aims to Reconcile AI and Copyright Law. China IP Network, May 28, 2025. https://ipr.mofcom.gov.cn/article/rgzhn/202505/1991749.html.

Users: Avoid prompting AI to generate infringing content and refrain from distributing potentially infringing AI-generated content.

In June 2024, the task force further proposed that the government or academic institutions act as intermediaries in licensing negotiations between collective management organizations and AI developers. It also suggested adding TDM exceptions to facilitate access to copyrighted content. Discussions on how AI developers can disclose training data lists to meet transparency obligations are ongoing.[30]

On December 26, 2024, South Korea's National Assembly passed the Basic Act on AI Development and Trust Building (hereafter referred to as the AI Basic Act), set to take effect on January 22, 2026. As the world's second country (after the EU) to enact foundational AI legislation, the Act focuses on both AI development and regulation to enhance industrial competitiveness. For training data copyright compliance, it emphasizes establishing a regulatory framework to prevent technology abuse and balance AI growth with copyright protection.

Article 31 of the AI Basic Act mandates enhanced transparency for AI systems, imposing three key obligations on operators of high-impact AI and generative AI products/services:

Notify users in advance that products/services rely on AI;
Clearly label AI-generated content to indicate its AI origin;
Prominently warn users of AI-generated audio/video that is indistinguishable from real content.

An exception allows adjusted notification methods for artistic/creative content to avoid disrupting appreciation. Article 43 further stipulates penalties for noncompliance with transparency obligations.

While countries and regions vary in their regulatory priorities and approaches, all are actively exploring frameworks tailored to generative AI—balancing technological innovation with copyright protection to foster the healthy, compliant development of the generative AI industry.

References

1. Ye C (2025) Regulation of copyright infringement in data "feeding" for generative artificial intelligence. Science Technology and Law Chinese-English Version 2:34
2. Linghan Z, He G, Xiaoqing F et al (2024) Symposium on copyright protection of AI-generated content (AIGC). Digital Law 1:11
3. Wenyi D, Dongmei X (2025) Copyright law responses to generative AI training data: a copyright compliance framework. Documentation,Information & Knowledge 1
4. Limei W, Qian W, Qian T et al (2024) Legal issues in the construction of artificial intelligence corpora. Digital Law 5:29

[30] Overview of Copyright Regulations for Generative AI Across Countries and Regions. Hubei Copyright Protection and Service Network, April 1, 2025. https://www.ccct.net.cn/html/bqzhisal/2025/0421/5980.html.

5. Handong W (2020) Copyright law questions on AI-generated works. Peking University Law Journal 3:656
6. Handong W (ed) (2014) Intellectual property law, 6th edn. Peking University Press
7. Sag M (2023) Copyright Safety for Generative AI. Houston Law Review 61:295
8. Guo D, Yunwei Z (2024) Infringement risks and legal responses of generative AI training data. Journal of Xiangtan University (Philosophy and Social Sciences):82
9. Jiangang S (2025) Copyright law analysis of data training. Legal Forum 2:69
10. Lili W (2025) The application choice of copyright restriction system in generative AI data training. Journal of Political Science and Law 5:162
11. Qi X (2018) Clarifying the judicial determination standards for copyright fair use. Law Science 1:182
12. Yifan L (2025) The copyright dilemma and outlet of generative AI data training behavior. Jianghai Academic Journal 4:185
13. Mingxuan L (2025) On the fair use of large model training data. The Jurist 5:33
14. Xinming C, Ye F (2024) Research on fair use rules for generative AI data training. China Copyright 4
15. Qi X, Wenyao Z (2024) Global trends and local paths of copyright regulation for AI-generated content. Intellectual Property 11:66
16. Qihang Z, Leilei J (2025) Information disclosure: a governance approach for the utilization of AI model training data. Library J:120
17. Da L (2024) Data risks of text-to-video artificial intelligence and their legal regulation—taking Sora as an example. Henan Social Sciences 10:82
18. Jieru J, He L (2025) Intellectual property regulatory Systems for Generative AI corpus training: overseas experience and implications. Journal of Modern Information 6
19. Daoqin D (2024) Data governance paths for the training phase of generative artificial intelligence. Administrative Law Review 6:21

Chapter 3
Copyright Ownership and Protection Boundaries of AI-Generated Content (AIGC)

This chapter focuses on the "output issue" of generative AI—namely, the legal characterization, right ownership, and protection scope of AIGC—addressing the core controversy of "whether AI-generated content is protected and who owns it."

3.1 Legal Characterization of AIGC: Whether It Constitutes a "Work" Under Copyright Law

Starting from the core requirement of "originality," this section analyzes the difficulties in determining AIGC's qualification as a work.

3.1.1 *The Criterion for "Originality": Human Creative Input Is Key*

The core of "originality" under copyright law lies in the requirement that a work must embody the "independent thinking and creative intellectual labor of the creator" (rather than mechanical reproduction or purely random generation).

First, a work refers to an intellectual achievement in the literary, artistic, or scientific domain that possesses originality and is expressed in a certain form. It is a unity of content and form, consisting of four constituent elements: belonging to the literary, artistic, or scientific domain; being created by an author; possessing originality; and being expressed in a certain form. A work must originate from the author itself and reflect a minimum degree of creativity. China's Copyright Law adopts the idea-expression dichotomy to define the scope of copyright protection: it protects expressions (i.e., the form in which intellectual achievements are manifested) rather

L. Cheng, *Copyright Issues Related to Generative Artificial Intelligence (AI)*, Artificial Intelligence and the Rule of Law,
https://doi.org/10.1007/978-981-95-8781-0_3

than abstract ideas. Therefore, the author's intellectual achievements must be expressed through a certain form—these achievements are the spiritual wealth protected by China's Copyright Law, and protecting the intellectual achievements and contributions embodied in works serves as an incentive for the regeneration of intellectual creation.

Originality requires independent creation. "Creation" refers to acts that directly determine expressive elements based on free will—such as the combination of words in literary works or postures, expressions, and movements in dance works. The requirement of "directness" mandates a close connection between the author and the work, excluding indirect involvement such as issuing instructions on the work's style or providing guidance and suggestions.

Originality is the core of work qualification. It requires independent creation (i.e., not copying or plagiarizing existing works of others) and the output of expressive elements based on free will—meaning intellectual input reflects personal choices and aesthetic expressions, and embodies a minimum degree of creativity. Specifically:

"Independence" means the work is distinct from existing works with recognizable differences;

"Creativity" means the author invests intellectual labor, presents the expressive content through a certain form, makes sufficient intellectual contributions that determine the nature of the expressive content, and the work meets the minimum threshold of creativity to reflect the creator's aesthetic choices and personal expression.

The criterion for originality is relatively abstract and relies on judicial authorities to refine review factors through case-by-case examination. The traditional originality standard applied to natural persons' works cannot be fully applied to AIGC. Due to the human-machine interactive nature of AIGC's generation process—where AI is not a simple auxiliary tool like a camera or brush—the determination of AIGC's originality should focus more on whether humans have made a minimum degree of contribution. Chinese courts adopt a relatively lenient approach to reviewing AIGC's originality, not requiring users to have perceptible control over the output content or to determine its expressive elements. Instead, they emphasize the degree of participation in labor contributions, such as repeatedly revising prompts or setting parameters, rather than whether the user ultimately determines the expressive elements of the AIGC output.

In natural persons' works, the transformation from idea to expression is direct, and natural persons have control over the expressive content. In AIGC works, the user's ideas (i.e., prompts) must be processed by AI to form the final expression. The complexity of this technical path has transformed the single output process from idea to expression. Therefore, the determination of AIGC's originality should assess the complexity of the technical path and the degree to which the user's input prompts determine and control the expressive elements of the output content.

It is important to distinguish between "creativity" and "originality": creativity refers to the nature of the work itself, while originality refers to the nature of the author's contribution to the work. A work must include the contribution of human intellectual labor. Originality not only depends on the author's contribution to the work but also on the nature of that contribution—whether it endows the work with distinctive attributes and establishes a close normative connection between the author and the work to achieve the specification of the right subject from a legal perspective.

The UK's Copyright, Designs and Patents Act 1988 (CDPA) stipulates the criterion for determining the originality of computer-generated works. Section 9(3) of the CDPA provides that for a literary, dramatic, musical, or artistic work generated by a computer, the author shall be deemed the person who made the necessary arrangements for the creation of the work.[1] Here, "necessary arrangements" refer to substantive contributions, and copyright protection for computer-generated works still requires consideration of originality. EU legal interpretations of Section 9(3) emphasize that "skill, effort, and time" alone are insufficient; instead, creativity and the author's intellectual input are required for AI-generated works to obtain copyright protection.[2]

Judicial standards for determining AIGC's originality vary across countries, focusing on differences in the required degree of human user contribution and control over the expressive elements of the output content. Initially, Chinese courts focused on reviewing originality based on the creative result—examining whether it maintained recognizable differences from existing works. Currently, all countries assess originality based on the creative process, requiring plaintiffs to bear the burden of proving sufficient intellectual input during creation and to provide documented operational procedures. This paper advocates assessing AIGC's originality during the creative process and adopting the subjective theory of originality for such determinations.

The U.S. Copyright Office's Copyright Registration Guidance[3] clarifies that, based on the Copyright Office's understanding of existing generative AI, users do not have ultimate creative control over how the system interprets instructions and generates content—instead, the machine determines how to execute these instructions in the output.[4] In the case of Zaria v. Dawn, the author was only granted rights of coordination, selection, and arrangement rather than full copyright. Even repeated revisions to prompts only influence (rather than determine) the expressive elements of the output content; users' general instructions are not commands, and they lack ultimate control over the output.

Currently, all countries adhere to the human authorship principle in determining AIGC's originality. The purpose of copyright law is to ensure that human authors obtain spiritual and material benefits from their works and to incentivize their

[1] Section 9(3), Copyright, Designs and Patents Act 1988 (CDPA).

[2] Sögüt Atilla: Regulating AI-Generated Works: Insights from UK Copyright Law, WeChat Official Account "International IP Observer", January 26, 2025.

[3] Copyright Registration Guidance: Works Containing Material Generated by Artificial Intelligence, 88 Fed. Reg. 16,190 (Mar. 16, 2023).

[4] Copyright and Artificial Intelligence, Part 2: Copyrightability, A Report of the Register of Copyrights (Jan. 29, 2025).

enthusiasm for re-creation. Under this principle, works originate from human authors, but copyright does not necessarily belong to the author—separation between authorship and copyright ownership can be achieved through commissioned creation or works made for hire relationships. Therefore, whether AIGC can qualify as a work protected by copyright depends on whether it meets the requirement of originality.

As a relatively abstract and vague standard, AIGC's originality requires more specific criteria for identification. Chinese courts have gradually established judicial standards for determining AIGC's originality and copyright through case-by-case reviews. For example:

In China's first AI text-to-image infringement dispute, Li v. Liu (titled "The Spring Breeze Brings Tenderness"), the Beijing Internet Court held that although the AI user generated the at-issue images through an AI generative platform, they had set numerous positive and negative prompts for the images' style and size, continuously adjusted parameters during generation, and ultimately formed the images—reflecting the user's personal aesthetic expressions and choices. The AI user documented the creative process and demonstrated the reproduction of the images to the court, showing that omitting any single instruction would have resulted in a different image. Therefore, the court ruled that the images possessed originality, qualified as works, and were protected by copyright. The judge noted that the originality of such works still requires case-by-case review. Only the original parts of a work are within the scope of copyright protection, which indirectly affects the amount of compensation for infringement.

In Lin v. Hangzhou XX Air Film Technology Co., Ltd. (the "Banxin" case) heard by the Changshu Court in Jiangsu Province, an AIGC designer used Midjourney and Photoshop to generate the final two-dimensional artistic pattern (named "Banxin") by continuously revising prompts and editing AI-generated images. The two defendants produced three-dimensional installations highly similar to the "Banxin" pattern. The plaintiff disclosed the documented generation process to the court, showing that their revisions during creation were only focused on the half-heart pattern in the water, while other prompts remained almost unchanged. Additionally, as hearts are common patterns and lack originality in themselves, the plaintiff's copyright was limited to the two-dimensional artistic work "Banxin" rather than the three-dimensional installation of the half-heart.

In the "Butterfly Transparent Chair" case heard by the Suzhou Intermediate Court, the court ruled that the butterfly transparent chair did not constitute a work under copyright law because the author could not reproduce the image.[5] The plaintiff claimed to have used the same prompts as during the original creation to reproduce the image, but due to the uncontrollability and randomness of generative artificial intelligence (GAI), they could not control the expressive elements of the output content. The court held that GAI played a decisive and controlling role in the

[5] CSLawyer Haitai Law Firm: Copyrightability and Right Ownership of AIGC in China, WeChat Official Account "The Path of Legal AGI", September 29, 2025.

image creation, making it difficult to conclude that the natural person's intellectual input determined the final expression.

Chinese courts initially adopted the tool theory, which holds that AI actors lack independent consciousness and are tool models designed by developers to exhibit human-like thinking through data training. Natural persons, as legal subjects, use generative AI as a tool to assist in creating works. Some domestic courts have ruled that content generated by users through multi-round linear revisions using generative AI qualifies as works. The determination of originality for such content has sparked a debate between the free will determination theory and the user originality contribution theory:

The free will determination theory argues that creation is an act where humans determine expressive elements based on free will. During multi-round revisions, users cannot predict or determine the output content, as expressive elements are determined by AI's algorithms and data.

The user originality contribution theory holds that during multi-round linear revisions, users perform personalized processing on AI-generated content by setting and adjusting parameters and editing details, reflecting their personal expressions and aesthetic choices. Users make original contributions to the generated content and should enjoy copyright.

There is still a need to establish quantitative standards to determine AIGC's originality, particularly regarding the significance of the human author's intellectual contribution to the generated content and the degree of control and predictability over its expressive elements.

Controversies Over the "Originality" of AIGC

AI can be categorized into assistive generative AI and autonomous generative AI. Creation is an expression of human free will: content autonomously generated by AI constitutes purely AI-generated material, lacking human creative input and thus ineligible for copyright protection. In the case of A Recent Entrance to Paradise, the applicant's attempt to secure copyright protection under the work-made-for-hire doctrine failed. The painting was autonomously generated by AI, and the work-made-for-hire doctrine addresses copyright ownership rather than copyrightability. Since AI lacks human status and cannot be an "employee," the court ultimately ruled that the work was ineligible for copyright protection—due to its autonomous AI generation, the absence of the applicant's intellectual contribution, and the failure to meet the human authorship requirement.

For AI-assisted generative content, human intervention in the generation process (e.g., inputting prompts, setting parameters) reflects the user's desired expressive elements. Copyright eligibility is determined by evaluating the human's intellectual labor contribution, including the degree of intellectual input during creation, minimum creativity, and control over the expressive elements of the output. Accordingly, the following discussion on AIGC's originality focuses on assistive generative AI.

(1) Negative Views: AIGC Lacks "Human Creative Input" as It Is Generated by Models Based on Algorithms and Training Data

Scholars represented by Shou Bu argue that AIGC is not copyrightable. They classify AI into symbolic AI (interpretable and proficient in deductive reasoning) and connectionist AI (neural network systems proficient in inductive learning), noting that generative AI falls into the latter category, characterized by an unexplainable "black box" effect. The idea-expression dichotomy is a fundamental principle defining the scope of copyright protection, and AIGC's copyrightability requires certainty in the transformation from idea to expression. By analogy to the interpretability, predictability, and certainty of the idea-to-expression transformation in natural persons' works, Shou Bu argues that AIGC fails to meet these criteria: the input of ideas and the generation of expressions lack mutual certainty—ideas cannot predict outputs (unpredictability), and outputs cannot be traced back to explain inputs (unexplainability).[6]

Scholars represented by Wang Qian also contend that AIGC lacks originality, refuting arguments supporting copyrightability such as the objective theory of originality, the creative tool theory, the investment incentive theory, and the constructive author theory. They emphasize that generative AI's black box effect results in an opaque creation process: identical prompts may produce different expressions, and users' prompts cannot determine the expressive elements of the output—meaning users lack control over the creation process.[7] Furthermore, selecting AI-generated materials, conducting multi-round revisions, or adjusting prompts does not reflect the user's creative personality; selection merely reflects passive acceptance of AI outputs, and multi-round revisions do not give users decisive control over the generation process.

(2) Affirmative Views: AIGC Can Reflect "Human Creativity" If Users Deeply Participate in the Generation Process Through "Detailed Prompts," "Multiple Parameter Adjustments," and "Post-Editing"

Arguments supporting AIGC's originality include the subjective theory of originality, objective theory of originality, creative tool theory, constructive author theory, and investment incentive theory.

Subjective vs. Objective Theories of Originality.

The debate between subjective and objective standards of originality has long existed:

The subjective theory focuses on the creative process, examining whether the author's aesthetic expressions and personal choices are reflected from the author's perspective. Heavily reliant on judges' aesthetic judgments and personal views, it was initially applied to the copyright protection of artistic works but is less conducive to protecting commercial works.

---

[6] Shou Bu. AI-Generated Content: Copyrightability and Copyright Holder Issues. Science Technology and Law Chinese-English Version), 2024(4).

[7] Qian [1].

The objective theory focuses on the result, evaluating originality based on the creativity of the output from the reader's perspective. It emphasizes the product of labor, arguing that labor resulting in a work constitutes creation. Proponents criticize the subjective theory's limitations in examining the author's intellectual input and aesthetic expressions during creation, citing the irreversibility of time as an obstacle to verifying the author's original intent and creative efforts. In response, the subjective theory argues that proving the user's intellectual input during creation should rely on normative reproduction (e.g., documenting operational procedures to reproduce the content) rather than factual reproduction, which suffices to meet the burden of proof for AIGC's originality.

The objective theory advocates for an objective criterion centered on the inherent value of the work, treating human creation as a non-essential element. It holds that as long as a work is independently completed and significantly different from existing works, it possesses originality even without human contribution. Proponents argue that content meeting the minimum threshold of creativity and fulfilling public needs—providing value equivalent to human-created works—should receive equal copyright protection, regardless of whether it originates from human creation. However, Locke's labor theory of property emphasizes that only human intellectual achievements (not naturally occurring) embody labor and intellectual contributions. The objective theory's sole focus on results leads to overly simplistic considerations, ultimately relying on judges' subjective judgments and becoming a disguised subjective theory.

Scholars represented by Wang Qian argue that the objective theory contradicts legal logic. In the "monkey selfie case," although the monkey's selfie met the criteria of significant difference and aesthetic value for a photographic work, it lacked human creative contribution and failed to meet the human authorship principle—upheld by most countries, which have not recognized AI as a copyright subject. Furthermore, the purpose of copyright law is to protect human intellectual achievements, incentivizing creativity through rewards for distribution, reproduction, and licensing. Animals like monkeys cannot benefit from this incentive mechanism, and protecting their accidental creations violates constitutional provisions on fundamental rights subjects. U.S. courts rejected the objective theory in A Recent Entrance to Paradise: Dr. Stephen Thaler applied for copyright registration for a painting titled A Recent Entrance to Paradise generated by his "Creativity Machine" AI, naming the AI as the author and himself as the copyright holder. The U.S. Copyright Office denied registration based on the human authorship principle, and the court upheld this decision on appeal. It ruled that machines cannot be original authors, cannot execute signatures to transfer copyright, and the purely machine-generated painting—lacking human creative input—was ineligible for copyright protection and should enter the public domain.

Debates Over Originality Standards: Tool Theory, Contribution Theory, and Determination Theory

(1) Creative Tool Theory

This theory holds that humans determine the expressive elements of the output, and AI merely serves as a creative tool—a means for human creation that cannot participate in deciding expressive elements. It argues that as long as a connection exists between the intellectual input of AI developers/users and the AI-generated content, the content should be deemed to originate from the developers/users, regardless of how tenuous the connection may be. However, this view incorrectly attributes originality to AIGC even without human intellectual input, violating the minimum creativity requirement for originality under China's Copyright Law and downplaying the importance of labor contributions. A low threshold for originality would overly expand the scope of copyright protection, restricting future creation. If simple prompt input constitutes creation, thousands of works lacking human creativity could be "produced" in a short period, triggering numerous copyright infringement disputes and overburdening courts. Technically, existing interactive GAI models have limited databases and operate as probabilistic models—frequent input of identical prompts is likely to yield similar outputs. This theory underestimates AI's participation in creation: the black box effect leads to unpredictable "blind box" outputs, where the user's input ideas may be irrelevant to the final expression, which is solely determined by AI. Such outputs lack the certainty of idea-to-expression transformation and cannot be equated to natural persons' works.

(2) Constructive Author Theory

This theory establishes a virtual legal personality for the intellectual property protection of AI-generated content, using legal fiction to treat AI (or its investors, developers, or managers) as legal "authors"—following the historical logic of recognizing legal persons as authors. By endowing AI or its stakeholders with legal subject status, the theory deems their "creation" as original works. Wang Qian criticizes this approach as putting the cart before the horse: originality determination and authorship are distinct categories. Originality is the core requirement for a work, while authorship determines copyright ownership under copyright norms. Only content meeting originality and other formal requirements qualifies as a work, after which ownership is addressed—these two steps cannot be conflated.

(3) Investment Incentive Theory

This theory argues that AIGC is original and that copyright should belong to developers. Generative AI operates under an economic mechanism distinct from the film industry: developers profit by offering paid AI creation services or embedding AI models in websites to increase traffic and convenience. However, assigning copyright to developers is irrelevant to incentivizing AI model investment and development. It would restrict users' usage rights, violating service agreements with paying users, reducing AI model usage and data input, hindering model training and improvement, and ultimately lowering developers' economic benefits. Separating copyright ownership (developers) and usage rights (users) would add unnecessary licensing procedures. While developers hold copyright in the AI model itself due to their intellectual input in development, they do not participate in the creative process (idea formation, input, or expression generation), lack intellectual input in

AIGC, and cannot predict or control the output's expressive elements. Thus, AIGC copyright should not belong to model developers.

(4) Three theories dominate debates over AIGC's originality standard:

The tool theory denies AI's subjectivity, emphasizing its role as an auxiliary tool without considering the proportion of human intellectual contribution. It is no longer adaptable to the development of GAI technology, as modern generative AI—neural network systems with strong independent learning and induction capabilities—exceeds the scope of a mere "tool."

The contribution theory examines the degree of human intellectual input in the work's generation. However, it is practically difficult to prove that human original expression constitutes the primary contribution, and its operational standards are vague.

The determination theory focuses on whether human authors have control and predictability over the expressive elements of AIGC outputs.

Given the limitations of the tool and contribution theories, the determination theory is advocated for AIGC originality assessment, focusing on users' control over the expressive elements of generated content.[8]

3.1.2 Differences in Work Qualification Among Different Types of AIGC

Purely AI-Generated Content Is Usually Not Recognized as a Work

Purely AI-generated content—such as text directly generated after inputting a simple prompt like "write a poem about spring"—is typically not deemed a work.

Generated randomly by AI without human intellectual input, such content fails to meet the originality requirement. Simple prompts constitute abstract ideas, and copyright law protects expressions rather than ideas themselves. While simple prompts may reflect the user's expressive expectations, they exert no control over the generated expressive content. Copyright law does not protect mechanically generated content without human intervention—for example, inputting advisory instructions rather than definitive commands. The more specific the prompt, the clearer the AI system's understanding of the user's intent, and the closer the output will be to the user's desired expression. In contrast, vague, general prompts make it difficult for the system to discern the user's ideal style, structure, or other expressive elements. Coupled with AI's black box effect, the AI often directly determines the work's structure, text, style, and aesthetic choices, controlling the expressive elements of the output.

[8] Yiheng and Zheng [2], pp. 36–44.

Human beings lack effective intervention in the AI generation process (e.g., setting parameters, modifying local details, or revising prompts repeatedly). Even assuming such interventions could constitute originality, simple advisory instructions result in an overly tenuous connection between humans and the output—unlike detailed positive/negative prompts or parameter adjustments that guide AI toward the user's preferred style. For example, the U.S. rejected the copyright registration application for the autonomously AI-generated painting A Recent Entrance to Paradise.

Human-Machine Collaborative Content May Be Recognized as a Work

Human-machine collaborative content—such as a script where the user provides "character settings and plot frameworks," which the AI generates and the user then revises—may qualify as a work.

The originality of human-machine collaborative content depends on two factors: the degree of human control over the expressive elements and the complexity of the technical path. While purely AI-generated content is evaluated for the presence of human intervention, collaborative content is assessed for the level of human intellectual contribution on the basis of existing intervention.

In China's first AIGC infringement case, Li v. Liu ("The Spring Breeze Brings Tenderness"), the court adopted the tool theory. It ruled that repeated prompt revisions, parameter adjustments, and the ability to document and reproduce the creation process demonstrated that humans used AI as an auxiliary tool to produce intellectual achievements—thus satisfying originality and qualifying as a protected work under copyright law.

In contrast, the U.S. adopts a stricter stance on AIGC copyright protection. It argues that "repeated prompt revisions," while reflecting human-machine interaction and certain labor contributions, do not constitute sufficient intellectual input to directly influence or determine the output's expressive elements. The machine remains the dominant force in the creation process, and thus such content lacks originality. Additionally, in multi-round revision scenarios:

In the first round, the user's prompt does not allow predictability of the output, nor does it meet the minimum creativity requirement.

In subsequent rounds, the user modifies parameters or manually edits the previous output, acting as a "harvester" who selects content from the AI's output pool without gaining predictability or control over the final result.

The U.S. Copyright Office maintains that such content lacks originality: repeated revisions merely approximate the user's ideal output, confirming that the initial generation process fails to fix the user's ideas into a stable expression. Humans lack control over the final output's expressive elements, and "harvesting" from AI-generated content pools is not copyrightable.

Data-Driven AIGC Usually Does Not Constitute a Work

Data-driven AIGC—such as AI-generated market analysis reports—typically does not qualify as a work due to the lack of "creativity."

Data-driven AIGC involves mere arrangement and combination of data, failing to reflect human aesthetic choices or personal expression. In Beijing Feilin Law Firm v. Baidu Inc.,[9] the plaintiff searched 2589 court judgments in the Weiku Xianxing database using keywords such as "film," "trial court," and "trial date," then clicked "visualization" to generate graphs (e.g., curves, bar charts, pie charts) presenting statistical data from multiple dimensions. This process—filtering and extracting data to form new datasets for multi-dimensional analysis—amounted to research-oriented rearrangement of existing data. The user made no new creative contributions, nor did the output reflect personal selective expression similar to a compiled work; it merely re-presented data in existing dimensions, thus failing to qualify as a work. The plaintiff's data report was generated by inputting keywords and selecting a generation mode in the AI tool, and could be replicated by any user—demonstrating no condensation of the plaintiff's intellectual achievements.

3.1.3 *Recognition Practices of Major Global Jurisdictions*

U.S. Standards for Determining AIGC Originality

The U.S. applies strict requirements for AIGC originality, focusing on whether the user has control over the expressive elements of the output. In its January 19, 2025 report Copyrightability of AIGC, the U.S. Copyright Office clarified that copyright protection does not extend to purely AI-generated material or content where humans exercise insufficient control over expressive elements—including content generated from simple prompts, highly detailed prompts, or repeated prompt revisions. Protecting such content would effectively grant copyright to ideas themselves, violating the idea-expression dichotomy and creating idea monopolies that hinder intellectual innovation.

(1) Purely AI-Generated Material Lacks Originality

Upholding the human authorship principle, purely AI-generated material is not recognized as a work. In Thaler v. Perlmutter,[10] Stephen Thaler invented the generative AI "Creativity Machine," which autonomously generated the painting A Recent Entrance to Paradise based on algorithms. Thaler applied for copyright registration naming the AI as the author and himself as the copyright holder, without modifying the AI-generated work. The court rejected the application, ruling that the purely

---

[9] Beijing Feilin Law Firm v. Beijing Baidu Netcom Technology Co., Ltd., Civil Judgment of Beijing Intellectual Property Court, (2019) Jing 73 Min Zhong No. 2030.

[10] Thaler v. Perlmutter, No. 23–5233, 2025 WL 1103843 (D.C. Cir. Mar. 18, 2025).

machine-generated painting lacked human creative input and failed to meet the human authorship requirement.

(2) Content Generated from Highly Detailed Prompts Lacks Originality

In Théâtre D'opéra Spatial, Jason Allen used the AI tool Midjourney, inputting at least 624 text prompts to generate an initial image. He then used Adobe Photoshop to remove flaws and add visual elements, and Gigapixel AI to enhance resolution and size—eventually creating a 2D artistic image for copyright registration. The court denied the application, ruling that highly detailed prompts do not enable users to control how AI processes and implements the prompts. Subsequent image processing merely eliminated defects and improved clarity, without adding creative elements. Regardless of prompt detail, the lack of sufficient human control prevents AI users from being recognized as authors. Prompts only convey unprotected abstract ideas, and AI's black box effect means identical prompts may yield different expressions—further confirming that prompt input alone does not demonstrate control over expressive elements. Copyright protects human intellectual achievements, not mere time and effort; repeated prompt revisions do not confer copyrightability.

(3) Limited Protection for Content with Perceptible Human Input

Copyright protection is granted when the input contains perceptible expressive elements, the output reflects original human expression, and human and AI contributions are distinguishable. In the Rose Enigma case, the author input hand-drawn illustrations that defined the perceptible output scope—providing a starting point, rough shape, and prototype for the output. The final work, Face of a Rose, fully embodied perceptible human expression, with a recognizable connection between the input sketch and the output. The U.S. Copyright Office carefully separated human and AI contributions, recognizing the originality of the human expression and protecting that portion of the work. Examples include inputs of personal audio, video, or manuscripts.

(4) Creative Selection, Coordination, and Arrangement of AI-Generated Material Qualifies for Protection

Human beings who creatively select, coordinate, and arrange AI-generated material may obtain copyright protection for the resulting integrated work. The core requirement is meeting the "three-stage creativity" standard: applicants must form original expression by "selecting, coordinating, and arranging" AI-generated material—exercising control over the expressive elements of the integrated work, analogous to the right of compilation under China's Copyright Law.

In A Single Piece of American Cheese,[11] Kent Keirsey used AI to generate multiple image materials, then integrated them into a collage through "selection,

[11] Zhao Xuanyi. Global Practices of AIGC Copyright Ownership from the A Single Piece of Cheese Copyright Registration Case. WeChat Official Account "Zhi Fa Zhuan Yan", November 19, 2025.

coordination, and arrangement" and applied for copyright registration. The Copyright Office initially rejected the application on the grounds that AI-generated content is not copyrightable, but approved it upon reconsideration. The purely AI-generated materials lacked copyrightability, but the applicant's creative selection, coordination, and arrangement of individual elements formed a new integrated work reflecting personal aesthetic choices—thus qualifying for overall copyright protection.

Similarly, U.S. artist Kristina Kashtanova created the sci-fi comic book Zarya of the Dawn, combining human-written dialogue with AI-generated images (created via Midjourney without modification). The Copyright Office granted registration for the entire work but limited protection to "the author's written text and the selection, coordination, and arrangement of AI-generated content," excluding the unprotectable pure AI-generated images.

China's Determination of AIGC Originality

Compared to the U.S., China adopts a relatively lenient standard for determining originality, with inconsistent judicial standards across regions. However, judicial criteria for originality are gradually becoming stricter and more professional, reflecting progress in China's judicial practice.

Courts initially adopted the tool theory, holding that humans use AI as an auxiliary tool to produce intellectual achievements—any human intervention, regardless of degree, would qualify AI-generated content as a work. However, modern AI's strong autonomy exceeds its tool-like attributes (unlike brushes or cameras), rendering the tool theory incompatible with AIGC originality evaluation.

In Feng v. Dongshan Company (copyright infringement and unfair competition case), the court ruled that the key to AIGC's work qualification lies in whether the user exercises substantive control and personalized selection over expressive elements. Although the plaintiff set concepts, refined keywords, input them into Midjourney, and screened initial images, they failed to provide complete records of the image generation process (via Midjourney and the image-editing app Xingtu) or original records of steps such as reference image selection and layer adjustments—thus the content was not recognized as a work.

In the "Butterfly Chair" case, the court emphasized that originality requires users to exercise substantive intervention in specific expressive elements (e.g., lines, colors, composition) rather than merely providing abstract ideas, marking a shift toward emphasizing control over expression.

In the "Guofeng Scroll Painting" case, the court held that originality depends on the user's control and predictability over expressive elements. Chinese courts have evolved from merely requiring human creation/intervention to emphasizing the degree of intervention—such as prompt detail, repeated prompt revisions, or parameter adjustments—focusing on the close connection between the user's creative acts and the final output.[12]

Key Judicial Precedents.

Li v. Liu ("The Spring Breeze Brings Tenderness") [(2023) Jing 0491 Min Chu No. 11279]: The court evaluated originality based on two criteria—independent completion and recognizable differences from prior works. It ruled that the plaintiff's intellectual input (conceptualization, prompt design, parameter setting) and documented reproduction of the creation process demonstrated independent completion and personal aesthetic expression, thus satisfying originality.

Li's StableDiffusion Case: The court held that works require "intellectual achievement" and "originality." Li's intellectual labor (prompt selection, parameter adjustment, repeated revision of outputs) reflected personal aesthetic choices and met the minimum creativity threshold, qualifying the content as a work.[13]

Butterfly Transparent Art Chair Case: Adopting the subjective theory of originality, the court examined whether the creation process reflected the user's aesthetic choices and personal expression. It denied originality because the "work" could be generated with a single initial prompt (no human intellectual input), and the randomness/uncontrollability of the generative AI platform prevented the plaintiff from reproducing the image using the same process. The court initially proposed that originality depends on the user's control over expressive elements and analyzed AI's black box effect as a cause of uncontrollability and unpredictability.

Banxin Case: The plaintiff generated four images via Midjourney, selected an ideal version, refined it through repeated prompt adjustments (quantity, shape, position), and re-input self-edited images to guide AI generation. The court recognized originality based on these iterative revisions, personalized selections, and user-edited inputs—contrary to the U.S. stance that repeated prompt revisions do not demonstrate control over expression.

Dreamwriter Case: The court conflated AI system copyright with AIGC copyright. Even developers cannot fully predict AI outputs or exercise absolute control; thus, they hold copyright in the AI system itself, not in the AI-generated content.

EU's Standard for Determining AIGC Originality

EU law has established the "Author's Own Intellectual Creation (AOIC)" standard for copyrightability through precedents, requiring works to reflect the author's personal expression and creative choices. For example:

---

[12] Chen Quwang. Copyright Determination and Platform Governance of AI-Generated Images: A Comparative Law Observation of China, the U.S., and the EU. WeChat Official Account "IP Frontline", August 26, 2025.

[13] Shi Taige, Zhang Fengming. Examining Key Points of Legal Protection for AIGC Through Typical Cases (Part 1): Judicial Practice and Adjudicative Logic of AIGC Copyright Determination. WeChat Official Account "Jingtian & Gongcheng Law Firm", May 19, 2025.

In Infopaq, the court ruled that "the selection, ordering, and combination of words" can constitute intellectual creation.

In Painer (photographic works), the court held that photographers' free and creative choices (e.g., shooting angle, lighting, composition, guiding the subject's expressions) qualify as intellectual creation.

While this foundational standard exists, there are no authoritative precedents for its specific application to AIGC. EU law has not clarified whether practices such as repeated prompt revisions, highly detailed prompts, parameter setting, or multi-round editing of AI-generated materials constitute "author's own intellectual creation."

EU copyright law consists of fragmented directives that member states must transpose into national law. The EU regulates AI technology macroscopically through the Artificial Intelligence Act (AI Act), which requires AI developers to disclose training data and the extent of AI involvement.[14]

3.2 Copyright Ownership of AIGC: Rules for Demarcating Right Holders

This section analyzes the right claims of AIGC's core participants (users, AI developers, and training data copyright holders) and sorts out the logic for determining ownership.

3.2.1 Right Claims and Legal Basis of Core Participants

Section 9(3) of the UK's Copyright, Designs and Patents Act 1988 (CDPA) stipulates: "In the case of a literary, dramatic, musical, or artistic work generated by a computer, the author shall be deemed to be the person by whom the necessary arrangements for the creation of the work were undertaken." Adhering to the human authorship principle, "the person by whom the necessary arrangements were undertaken" typically includes:

Developers: Entities that design algorithms, train models, and set generation rules (e.g., AI companies);

Users: Entities that input original instructions (e.g., complex prompts, parameter adjustments) that substantially influence the output.

The determination of right ownership depends on the closeness of the connection between the participant's creative acts and the expressive elements of the output.

When AIGC is copyrightable, the ownership is usually governed by the service contract between the user and the AI developer—"agreements prevail." Given the

[14] European Union. Artificial Intelligence Act (AI Act), July 2024.

service nature of AI developers, copyright typically belongs to users in practice. In the absence of an agreement, the ownership is determined by evaluating the degree of intellectual contribution, control over expressive elements, and connection to the creative content of both parties (users and developers) under the human authorship principle. If both parties exercise control over their respective closely connected contributions, co-ownership (joint or fractional) may be adopted. However, co-ownership is inefficient for utilizing intellectual property and requires a supporting profit-sharing mechanism.

Users Claim Copyright Belongs to Them, Arguing Prompts Are the Core of Creative Input

Users cannot claim copyright if they only participate through simple prompt input—copyright law does not protect abstract ideas, nor does it protect expressions that are the only or limited ways to convey an idea.

In Chinese judicial practice, courts recognize user ownership if the user:

Provides documented records to reproduce the AIGC creation process and results;

Iteratively refines the output through highly detailed positive/negative prompts or parameter adjustments, meeting the standard of intellectual input.

However, under the U.S. Copyright Registration Guidance for AIGC, users acting as "harvester authors" in multi-round generation scenarios are not entitled to copyright:

Content generated in the first round (simple prompt input) lacks copyrightability;

Subsequent rounds of parameter modifications, prompt adjustments, or manual edits do not confer copyrightability, as AI's inherent black box effect prevents users from predicting or controlling the output—users merely select the closest match from the AI's output pool.

AI developers often acknowledge that users contribute intellectually to creation and that user-generated outputs based on the model should belong to users. Restricting user ownership would severely limit user experience, harm the model's economic benefits, and contradict developers' market expectations. Nevertheless, some developers retain AIGC ownership through contractual agreements, excluding users' ownership rights.

AI Developers Claim Copyright Belongs to Them, Arguing the Model Is the Foundation of Content Generation

AI developers assert ownership on the grounds that the model is the foundational intermediary connecting users to works—AIGC generation requires both the AI model and user inputs (e.g., creative prompts, parameter settings), with neither being dispensable. However, this argument is flawed:

The model only serves as a generation tool; AIGC begins with the user's creative ideas and prompts, which developers and the model cannot predict.

Due to AI's black box effect (probabilistic model nature), developers cannot predict the output content—whether it replicates raw training data or transforms it, or the structure of data arrangement. Even if the model can autonomously generate AIGC without human intervention, developers lack control over the output's source or form.

Thus, developers' ownership of the model does not logically extend to ownership of AIGC.

Training Data Copyright Holders Claim Partial Rights, Arguing AIGC Derives from Knowledge Extracted from Training Data

Training data copyright holders are upstream in the development process, while AIGC is produced downstream in the creation phase. If developers are not entitled to claim copyright, training data holders have even weaker standing—extending the copyright protection chain excessively would unduly restrict third-party rights.

Key counterarguments to their claims include:

Weak connection to AIGC: Training data only realizes its value in model development through developers' intellectual labor (training, integration, screening). The model learns vector features and thinking patterns from data through transformative use, forming its own database. AIGC outputs have a tenuous connection to raw training data.

Technical and practical barriers: Developers source training data from diverse channels (web crawling, public data, user inputs, professional databases), making it technically infeasible and cost-prohibitive to verify the legality of each data source.

Inefficiency of co-ownership: Granting copyright to numerous training data holders would lead to ownership disputes and conflict with the economic principle of efficient single ownership.

Irrelevance to originality criteria: Training data holders do not participate in either the user's input/editing process or the AI system's technical path (e.g., black box effect)—the two core factors for determining AIGC originality and ownership.

Thus, training data copyright holders are not entitled to claim AIGC copyright.

3.2.2 Copyright Ownership Rules in Different Scenarios

Non-commercial Personal Use Scenario: Ownership Vests in Users for AIGC Generated for Personal Learning

Under Article 19 of the Copyright Law of the People's Republic of China, the ownership of commissioned works shall be agreed upon by the commissioning party and the commissioned party through a contract. Where there is no explicit agreement in the contract or no contract is concluded, the copyright shall belong to the commissioned party.

In commercial commissioning scenarios, where an enterprise commissions an AI service provider to generate AIGC, copyright ownership shall be determined by contract terms. The commissioning party is typically the enterprise user, and the commissioned party is the AI service provider. The separation of authorship and copyright ownership can be achieved through a commission contract, with ownership generally vesting in the commissioning enterprise user as agreed. In the absence of contractual terms, Article 19 of the Copyright Law stipulates that copyright shall belong to the commissioned party (i.e., the AI developer).

However, unlike natural-person works where the commissioned party's creativity directly shapes the work's expression, AIGC creation relies on the user's provision of creative ideas. If the commissioned party (AI service provider) only supplies the AI model without contributing creative concepts, rigidly applying Article 19 will lead to a misalignment between the party providing perceptible expressive elements and the copyright holder. Therefore, the determination of AIGC copyright ownership in commission contract relationships should comprehensively consider:

Whether the creative concept is provided by the commissioning party or the commissioned party;
Whether the concept exercises control over the expressive elements of the output;
Whether it reflects personal aesthetic choices and styles;
Whether the commissioned party has made qualitative modifications to the commissioning party's creative concept.

Work-for-Hire Scenario: Ownership Generally Vests in the Employer for AIGC Generated by Employees to Fulfill Job Duties

Article 11 of the Copyright Law of the People's Republic of China stipulates: "Copyright shall belong to the author, except as otherwise provided in this Law. The natural person who creates a work shall be the author. For a work created under the auspices of a legal person or unincorporated organization, representing the will of the legal person or unincorporated organization, and for which the legal person or unincorporated organization shall bear responsibility, the legal person or unincorporated organization shall be deemed the author."

Article 18 provides: "A work created by a natural person to fulfill the tasks of a legal person or unincorporated organization shall be a work for hire. Except as provided in the second paragraph of this Article, the copyright shall belong to the author, but the legal person or unincorporated organization shall have the priority to use the work within the scope of its business operations. Within two years after the completion of the work, the author shall not license a third party to use the work in the same manner as the entity uses it without the consent of the entity.In any of the following circumstances, the author shall enjoy the right of authorship, and other copyright rights shall belong to the legal person or unincorporated organization, which may reward the author:(1) A work for hire such as an engineering design drawing, product design drawing, map, schematic diagram, or computer software that is created mainly by using the material and technical conditions of the legal person or unincorporated organization and for which the legal person or unincorporated organization shall bear responsibility;(2) A work for hire created by the staff of a newspaper office, periodical office, news agency, radio station, or television station;(3) A work for hire for which the copyright shall belong to the legal person or unincorporated organization as provided by laws, administrative regulations, or as agreed in a contract."

Article 11 of the Implementing Regulations of the Copyright Law (2013 Revision) clarifies that the "job duties" referred to in Article 18, paragraph 1 of the Copyright Law mean the obligations that a citizen shall perform in the legal person or organization. Article 16, paragraph 2 of the Copyright Law states that the "material and technical conditions" referred to in the provisions on works for hire mean the funds, equipment, or materials specially provided by the legal person or organization for the citizen to complete the creation. Article 12 specifies that within 2 years after the completion of a work for hire, if the author licenses a third party to use the work in the same manner as the entity uses it with the entity's consent, the remuneration obtained therefrom shall be distributed between the author and the entity in accordance with the agreed ratio. The two-year period after the completion of the work shall be calculated from the date on which the author delivers the work to the entity.

For AIGC to be deemed a work for hire of a legal person or organization, it must meet three criteria: the creation is hosted by the employer, represents the employer's will, and the employer assumes liability for the work. For ordinary works for hire that do not fall into the three categories of special works for hire specified in Article 18, paragraph 2, copyright shall in principle belong to the employee-author. For special works for hire, the employee generates AIGC using AI, initially acquiring copyright, which is then transferred to the employer through the work-for-hire relationship.

To determine whether AIGC constitutes a work for hire of a legal person or an ordinary/special work for hire, the following factors shall be examined:

Whether the creation of AIGC is related to the employee's job duties;
Whether the job duties fall within the employer's business scope;
Whether the creation aligns with the employee's job responsibilities;
Whether it meets the conditions for special works for hire under Article 18, paragraph 2 of the Copyright Law.

If AIGC constitutes a work for hire of a legal person or a special work for hire, the employer shall own the copyright; if it constitutes an ordinary work for hire, the employee shall own the copyright.

Open-Source AI Scenario: Ownership Generally Vests in Users, Subject to Compliance with Open-Source Agreement Terms

An open-source AI model refers to an AI model that publicly discloses its model architecture, parameter weights, training methods, and partial data. Compared with closed-source models, open-source models feature complete, transparent code, avoiding the black box effect. Groups with high customization needs can participate in modifying the model's source code and setting parameters to generate AIGC, enabling a high degree of human-machine collaboration. The open algorithm process ensures that the transformation from idea to expression is interpretable, predictable, and deterministic. Users who input prompts and participate in source code modification can predict the output content and exercise decisive control over its expressive elements.

Furthermore, user feedback and technical contributions are crucial drivers of model iteration. To incentivize more users to participate in source code development, open-source agreements between model developers and users generally assign copyright to users, encouraging them to promote further iteration and upgrading of the open-source model.

3.2.3 Controversial Difficulty: Can AI Itself Be a Right Holder?

Legal Barriers: Global Copyright Laws Stipulate That "Right Holders Must Be Natural Persons, Legal Persons, or Unincorporated Organizations"—AI Lacks Legal Subject Qualification

Article 1 of China's Copyright Law stipulates the legislative purpose: "This Law is enacted in accordance with the Constitution for the purposes of protecting the copyright of authors of literary, artistic, and scientific works, as well as the rights and interests related to copyright, encouraging the creation and dissemination of works conducive to the construction of socialist spiritual civilization and material civilization, and promoting the development and prosperity of socialist culture and science." Article 2 provides: "Works of Chinese citizens, legal persons, or unincorporated organizations shall be protected by this Law, whether published or not."

The legislative purpose of the Copyright Law is to determine the ownership of intellectual property rights and protect human intellectual achievements, which is the foundation for incentivizing creation and legal dissemination. Enacted in accordance with the Constitution, it adheres to the principle of supremacy of higher-level laws and constitutionality, and cannot add non-human author subjects beyond the scope of right holders specified in the Constitution. Article 2 further clarifies the scope of author subjects, upholding the human authorship principle.

U.S. courts cite the text of the Copyright Act and historical precedents (e.g., Burrow-Giles Lithographic Co. v. Sarony), noting that an "author" must be a human being because the core purpose of copyright law is to "promote human creativity through economic incentives." They further elaborate on seven key points demonstrating that machines do not possess the attributes required of an "author" under the Copyright Act:

The ownership provisions of the Copyright Act are predicated on the author's legal capacity to own property;

The Copyright Act limits the term of copyright to the author's lifetime or a period approximating a human lifespan;

The inheritance provisions of the Copyright Act stipulate that upon the author's death, their "termination rights" shall be owned and exercisable by their "widow or widower" or "surviving children or grandchildren";

Copyright transfers require a signature;

Unpublished works are protected regardless of the author's nationality or place of residence;

Authors possess intent;

In contrast, every time the Copyright Act references machines, the context indicates that machines are tools, not authors.

Granting AI authorship status would violate the human authorship principle and contradict the legislative purpose of copyright laws worldwide. The legal fiction of AI as a legal subject is proposed to resolve issues of right ownership and liability bearing, but it not only fails to fully address these problems but also gives rise to new ones:

As a virtual entity without responsible property, how can AI assume tort liability? Ultimately, liability would fall on AI developers as the property-owning entities.

Current AI lacks independent will. For AI to participate in market transactions independently, license use by other market entities, and generate copyright revenue, it would still need to enter into licensing agreements through an agency relationship with AI developers.

The legal fiction of AI as a subject does not fundamentally resolve the issues of how it can exercise rights and perform obligations in legal relationships, and it increases the legislative difficulty of aligning AI with the systems of natural persons, legal persons, and unincorporated organizations under civil and copyright law. AI cannot be fully governed by the legal person system.

Liu Yun proposes conferring electronic person status on AI by fictionalizing it as an author, advocating the use of legal person fiction methods (e.g., foundation legal persons) or analogical application of civil and commercial agency relationships. However, this approach faces significant legislative challenges: traditional agency relationships require both principals and agents to be subjects with capacity for rights and conduct, and issues such as principal immunity for agent torts and ultra vires acts by agents present difficulties comparable to legislating AI subject status. The demand for granting AI legal subject qualification stems from the need for contractual capacity and profit-making capacity (copyright protection needs).

The mainstream view in copyright law holds that authors under copyright law can only be humans, and the incentive mechanism of copyright law targets human investment, not AI. Due to the uncontrollability and unpredictability of human-AI collaborative creation, and the tenuous connection between users and works, AI-generated content lacking human creativity is not protected and may enter the public domain. If fully autonomous, creative AI agents emerge in the future, they should be granted creator status, with their interests and control vested in their developers or users.

Alternative Proposals by some Scholars: "Establishing AI Trusts" or "Entrusting Developers to Hold AIGC Rights on AI's Behalf"—No Legislative Practice Supports these Proposals to Date

Establishing AI trusts—where AI developers act as trustees, AI as the settlor, and users as beneficiaries—aims to separate ownership and beneficial rights. While seemingly aligning with the AI industry's business model, this approach essentially nullifies AI's copyright as the developer-trustee would exercise de facto ownership. Developers would be obligated to act in the best interests of user-beneficiaries to safeguard the independence of AIGC copyright. However, AI lacks independent will and cannot entrust developers to act as trustees, making the establishment of such a trust relationship legally infeasible.

Most countries worldwide uphold the human authorship principle in their copyright laws, and AI cannot become a right holder due to the lack of legal personality. As developers who invest core intellectual and capital resources in AI model research and development, entrusting them to hold AI-related rights aligns with the mainstream legal theory of the tool approach. However, the scope of entrusted rights should be determined based on different theoretical perspectives:

Under the determination theory, developer trusteeship requires that developers exercise control over the AIGC creation process and determine the outcome. If developers only provide basic tools while users make original contributions through prompts and parameter adjustments, the entrusted rights should tilt toward users.

Under the contribution theory, developer trusteeship provides a framework for determining copyright ownership: if developers' screening and arrangement of AI outputs reach a creative level, they may hold complete copyright through trusteeship; if they only provide basic algorithm tools, the entrusted rights shall be limited to technology-related usage rights.

In addition, based on the principle of unifying rights and obligations, developers entrusted with holding rights must not only enjoy rights but also assume joint and several liability for torts arising from AI-generated content.

3.3 Protection Boundaries of AIGC: Scope of Rights and Infringement Determination

This section clarifies the scope of protection for AIGC and how to determine whether AIGC infringes the copyright of existing works.

3.3.1 *Scope of Copyright Protection for AIGC: Application of Moral Rights and Economic Rights*

Only when AIGC constitutes a work with a clear "creator" can it enjoy moral rights such as the right of authorship and the right of modification. The application of economic rights such as the right of reproduction, distribution, and information network dissemination to AIGC must be premised on not infringing the copyright of existing works.

Article 10 of China's Copyright Law stipulates 12 copyright rights, covering both moral rights and economic rights. Upholding the human authorship principle, the authors of AIGC works and natural-person works are both copyright holders as defined by the Copyright Law, and AIGC works shall enjoy the same scope of copyright protection as natural-person works.

The author of an AIGC work shall enjoy the moral rights and economic rights specified in Article 12 of China's Copyright Law, including the right to claim authorship, publish, modify, reproduce, and protect the integrity of the AIGC work; the right to publicly disseminate or broadcast the AIGC work; and the right to adapt or compile the AIGC work. They may license others to exercise economic rights such as reproduction, distribution, information network dissemination, and compilation for remuneration.

The transferability of AIGC's economic rights determines the restrictive nature of their protection: economic rights are subject to a time limit, and the principle of restrictive protection is adopted, with systems such as fair use, statutory licensing, and author-authorized licensing established to balance the interests of authors and the public interest. In contrast, the moral rights of AIGC authors are exclusive, non-transferable, and inalienable, and shall be protected for a longer period—usually in perpetuity—under the principle of absolute protection.

3.3.2 *Standards for Determining Copyright Infringement by AIGC*

The "access + substantial similarity" principle is the core standard for judging whether AIGC constitutes infringement.

Constitutive Elements of Infringement: Access + Substantial Similarity

(1) Judgment of the Access Element

The access element is satisfied by proving the existence of actual access or a high likelihood of access. Chinese courts determine the likelihood of access based on factors such as whether the work has been published, the publication platform, and the work's popularity. Access is a presumptive element: if a work has been previously published and enjoys high popularity, a high likelihood of access can be presumed. For unpublished works, the plaintiff shall bear the burden of proving that the defendant actually accessed the copyrighted work.[15] Substantial similarity is a probative element: if it can be proven that the content is highly similar to the substantive content of another's existing copyrighted work, the fact of access can be presumed.

(2) Judgment of the Substantial Similarity Element

In traditional Chinese judicial practice, the result comparison method is used to judge whether works constitute substantial similarity: when two comparable works exist, the court compares whether their substantive content is highly similar. Two main methods are applied:

Abstraction-Filtration-Comparison (AFC) Method: This method follows the steps of "abstraction, filtration, and comparison," focusing on the original, protectable parts of the work, excluding unprotected elements such as ideas, limited expressions, and public domain content, and only comparing whether the expressions are substantially similar. It provides a more objective comparison and is suitable for literary works and computer software works.

Total Concept and Feel (TCF) Method: Also known as the holistic perception method, it emphasizes overall recognition rather than item-by-item comparison of creative elements. It judges whether the core content and features of a work are similar to those of another's existing copyrighted work based on the intuitive inherent perception of an ordinary audience, and is suitable for photographic and artistic works.[16]

The traditional result comparison method for judging substantial similarity in paper-based textual works is no longer applicable to AIGC. Due to AI's black box effect, the generation process is opaque, making it impossible to determine the specific time point when the infringing result occurs. Clarifying whether the time point for establishing substantial similarity is at the result stage or the process stage is crucial for establishing the causality of infringement. Otherwise, the same prompt may generate different expressions through the AI technical path, leading to

[15] Wu Dacheng, Wang Qian. Trial Ideas for Copyright Infringement Cases. WeChat Official Account "Shanghai Higher People's Court", April 21, 2025.

[16] Zou Lin, Teng Mingcheng. Research on the Determination of Substantial Similarity in Architectural Works. WeChat Official Account "Copyright Theory and Practice", April 3, 2025.

uncertainty about whether the causality of infringement is established in the two generation processes.[17]

Academic circles have debated two approaches to judging the substantial similarity of AIGC:

Processualism (Technicalism): Emphasizes analyzing substantial similarity based on technical principles and advocates for the principle of technological neutrality to exempt liability for accidental substantial similarity. However, if processualism overemphasizes AI's black box effect, it will be difficult to establish substantial similarity, allowing users to evade liability through vague technical arguments regardless of whether infringement is actually constituted.

Resultism (Externalism): Does not consider AI's complex technical path and only compares whether there is a high degree of similarity in results. This approach ignores the uncertainty of establishing the causality of infringement during the generation process.

A more balanced approach is to divide AI output into defective output and ideal output when judging substantial similarity:

Defective output: Refers to coincidental situations where AI's technical vulnerabilities (e.g., data memorization) lead to the precise reproduction of the expressive content of existing works. Technicalism argues that the accidental reproduction of existing works due to objective technical vulnerabilities does not constitute infringement, but if AI developers are negligent in addressing such technical defects, they shall be liable for infringement.

Ideal output: Refers to output that meets developers' expectations, learning styles that are not protected under copyright law. Resultism advocates for analyzing results using traditional methods, adhering to the idea-expression dichotomy to prevent finding infringement based on high stylistic similarity.[18]

(3) Substantial Similarity Occurs at Both the Input and Output Stages

AIGC infringes on existing works mainly by using existing works as training data to generate derivative works without the authorization of the copyright holder. This can be divided into two scenarios: input data infringement and output content (derivative work) infringement.

Input Data Infringement.

The data training phase of AI model development includes data collection, labeling, filtering or transformation, data input, model training, and large model deep learning. Data sources are diverse, including publicly available data, crawled data, data purchased from databases, or data used under licensing agreements with databases. Due to the volume and diversity of data, verifying the legality of each data source is time-consuming and unfeasible, and AI developers cannot be imposed with an excessive obligation to review data source legality. However, ensuring the legality of data sources is a prerequisite for non-infringement.

[17] Shilin and Cheng [3], pp. 15–27.

[18] Huibin and Huaibin [4].

Even if data is sourced from public channels or web crawling, the purpose of using data for AI training is not reproduction for reproduction's sake. Large models extract vector features from datasets, learning non-expressive elements such as grammatical structures, arrangements, and thinking patterns—rather than copying expressive content. Data often undergoes a transformative phase during training, evolving into new data that constitutes transformative use.

The concept of "transformative use" was first proposed by U.S. Judge Pierre Leval in his 1990 Harvard Law Review article Toward a Fair Use Standard, where he defined it as follows: "If the original work is used as material to add new information, new aesthetics, new observations, and understandings, thereby adding new value to the original work, it constitutes fair use and is a typical type of behavior that needs to be protected for the public interest".[19]

U.S. courts judge whether conduct constitutes "fair use" by evaluating four factors:

The purpose and character of the use;
The nature of the copyrighted work;
The amount and substantiality of the portion used in relation to the copyrighted work as a whole;
The effect of the use upon the potential market for or value of the copyrighted work.[20]

Key considerations include whether the use is for reproduction, whether the data is reproduced and disseminated to users, whether it is used for commercial purposes, whether the data itself is protected by copyright, and whether it dilutes the market for existing and future works. Among the four factors, the nature of the copyrighted work and the amount/substantiality of the portion used carry less weight in the comprehensive assessment, serving mainly as auxiliary factors for judging other elements. Even if a large portion of the copyrighted work is used, if it can be proven that the purpose and character of the use are non-commercial and do not cause market dilution, it shall be deemed fair use and not substantially similar.

Transformative use of training data generally does not cause market dilution: the higher the degree of data transformation, the lower the degree of substitution for the original work, and the smaller the impact on the original work's potential and future markets. Under the principle of "he who asserts must prove," the infringed party claiming infringement bears the burden of proof, which is generally difficult given the need to demonstrate market dilution of the original work. To prove market dilution, it is first necessary to define market boundaries to predict the scope of the potential market—comprehensively using market research, online platform data monitoring, expert evaluation, industry analysis reports, etc., to analyze changes in the original work's market share, commercial revenue, consumer demand, and dissemination channels. If the original work's market share declines significantly,

[19] Leval [5], p. 1105.

[20] U.S. Court Issues First Ruling That AI Training Constitutes Fair Use. WeChat Official Account "International Intellectual Property Observer", June 29, 2025.

copyright licensing revenue or direct sales revenue decreases, or consumer attention or purchase intent for the original work drops noticeably after AIGC enters the original work's market, there may be a risk of market harm. It is necessary to further clarify the specific weight of each of the four factors in the comprehensive judgment to enhance the operability of judicial adjudication and help AI developers predict the infringement risks of training data in advance.

Legislative Trends on Text and Data Mining (TDM) Exceptions

UK: The Copyright, Designs and Patents Act 1988 permits text and data mining of copyrighted works for non-commercial purposes, provided that users have lawful access to the works (e.g., through subscription or licensing). In a consultation paper released in December 2024, the UK government stated that it deems it necessary to amend copyright law in the context of AI, proposing to expand the existing TDM exception to allow commercial use, provided that "right holders have not opted out of such use of their works."

EU: The 2019 Copyright Directive in the Digital Single Market[21] sets specific exceptions for text and data mining (including AI training), but their application is strictly limited to non-commercial use by research institutions. The DSM Directive establishes a TDM exception that covers most commercial AI training activities while providing a mechanism for copyright holders to reserve their rights.

Japan: According to government opinions, TDM provisions allow the use of copyrighted works for AI training, provided that it does not cause "unreasonable harm" to the interests of copyright holders.

Israel: Although there is no specific exception for TDM, the Ministry of Justice has issued clear opinions stating that most machine learning training scenarios can rely on existing exceptions in copyright law (such as fair use, incidental use, and temporary reproduction exceptions) to conduct TDM.

Countries around the world have gradually established TDM exceptions, with international legislative principles for TDM exceptions falling into three categories:

Broad exceptions: Countries such as the EU, Japan, Singapore, and Israel recognize TDM as a general exception to copyright law, allowing extensive use while establishing mechanisms to protect the rights of copyright holders.

Limited exceptions: Countries such as the UK and Switzerland limit TDM exceptions based on the purpose of TDM, particularly restricting commercial use.

Reliance on existing frameworks: Countries such as the U.S., Australia, South Korea, and New Zealand have not established specific exceptions for TDM, mainly relying on existing copyright frameworks such as fair use or temporary reproduction systems. Notably, jurisdictions without specific TDM exceptions have also gradually included TDM copyright issues in policy, legislative, and judicial discussions.[22]

---

[21] Directive (EU) 2019/790 of the European Parliament and of the Council of 17 April 2019 on copyright and related rights in the Digital Single Market and amending Directives 96/9/EC and 2001/29/EC, OJ L 130, 17.5.2019, p. 92–125.

[22] DataLaw Frontier Observer. Observation | International Data Governance Dynamics (1): Diverse Paths and Evolutionary Trends of Copyright Regulation for Text and Data Mining (TDM). WeChat Official Account "DataLaw Frontier Observer", March 15, 2025.

Fair Use of Training Data in China.

Before the third revision of the Copyright Law, China's fair use system adopted a closed-list approach, specifying 12 scenarios that did not include the use of data for AI model training, failing to adapt to the development of the internet industry. After the third revision, the legislative trend was further liberalized, adding a catch-all provision: "other circumstances as provided by laws and administrative regulations." It is necessary for subsequent administrative regulations or other legal norms to stipulate the use of training data for AI model development as fair use, forming a limitation on the rights of existing works.

In 2011, the Supreme People's Court's Opinions on Giving Full Play to the Functions of Intellectual Property Trials to Promote the Great Development and Prosperity of Socialist Culture and the Independent and Coordinated Development of the Economy[23] pointed out: "In special circumstances truly necessary for promoting technological innovation and commercial development, considering factors such as the nature and purpose of the work use behavior, the nature of the used work, the quantity and quality of the used portion, and the impact of the use on the potential market or value of the work, if the use behavior neither conflicts with the normal use of the work nor unreasonably harms the legitimate interests of the author, it may be deemed fair use." The Opinions integrate the three-step test with the four-factor test specified in Section 107 of the U.S. Copyright Act[24] to judge fair use.

In Chinese judicial practice, courts adopt three methods to judge fair use:

Three-step test: Fair use is only permitted in certain special circumstances (e.g., personal study, research, appreciation, or news reporting); it shall not conflict with the normal use of the work and shall not unreasonably harm the legitimate interests of the right holder.

U.S. four-factor test.

Transformative use based on the U.S. four-factor test.

The diversity of fair use judgment methods has led to inconsistent rulings in similar cases in judicial practice.[25] Clarifying the fair use judgment method is crucial for unifying judicial adjudication standards.

Representative Cases on Training Data Infringement.

Germany: OpenAI Infringement Case: In 2024, GEMA (Germany's largest collective management organization for musical work copyrights) filed a lawsuit with the Munich Regional Court, accusing OpenAI of using a large number of

[23] Opinions on Giving Full Play to the Functions of Intellectual Property Trials to Promote the Great Development and Prosperity of Socialist Culture and the Independent and Coordinated Development of the Economy, Fa Fa〔2011〕No. 18, issued on December 16, 2011.[89] 17 U.S.C. § 107.

[24] 17 U.S.C. § 107.

[25] Yang Xiangyu. Dilemmas and Solutions of the Copyright Fair Use System in the Digital Age. Intelligent Rule of Law, Vol. 3, 2023—Research Collection on the Legal Guarantee for Promoting Educational Digitalization.

copyrighted song lyrics owned by its members to train the ChatGPT model without authorization or compensation. The court held that both data memorization during training and the reproduction of lyrics in output content constituted substantial similarity, rejecting OpenAI's fair use defense. It ruled that even transformative use cannot completely circumvent copyright licensing requirements, especially when AI systems can output content substantially similar to the original work. The court further prohibited OpenAI from using copyrighted materials managed by GEMA for AI training without authorization. Adopting a traditional copyright protection perspective, the court brought both the input and output stages within the scope of copyright protection. The Munich court's strict definition of transformative use and fair use will prompt AI companies to re-evaluate their data collection and training strategies and establish more robust copyright compliance systems.[26]

U.S. Attitude: The U.S. adopts a lenient stance on training data copyright issues, highly relying on the fair use principle. In addition, transformative use—adding new information, aesthetics, and expressions to the original work, or even creating content completely different from the original data—and non-expressive use—extracting vector features of data rather than expressive content—are both not intended for reproduction, and do not reproduce the original data to users. Even developers may not know the form of data transformation during model training. The stronger the "transformative nature" of the work use, the weaker the "substantive substitutability" for the original work, and the smaller the impact on the original work's potential market and value, thus not substantially harming the rights of the original work's author.

Infringement at the Output Stage

Infringement at the output stage occurs when AIGC generates content that is substantially similar to existing copyrighted works. Due to the characteristics of AI's technical path, the likelihood of access can often be presumed.

The judgment of "substantial similarity" in AIGC copyright infringement cannot be analogously applied to the result comparison method used for natural-person works. Currently, mainstream judgment methods include the abstraction-filtration-comparison method, ordinary observer test, total concept and feel method, and internal-external test method, but all have certain limitations: the abstraction-filtration-comparison method compares AIGC with the allegedly infringed work item by item, while the total concept and feel method compares AIGC as a perceptible whole with the allegedly infringed work in terms of style and core features.

The static result comparison method for judging the substantial similarity of natural-person works in traditional print and online dissemination environments is insufficient to determine the certainty of the causality of infringement between

[26] Key Disputes and Legal Analysis of the First AI Training Data Copyright Case in Europe. WeChat Official Account "International Commercial Dispute Resolution", November 17, 2025.

input data and output content in AIGC. Clarifying the time point when substantial similarity is constituted—i.e., when and at which stage the substantially similar content is generated—is crucial for judging the establishment of infringement. The technical mechanism of the black box effect makes the occurrence of infringing results accidental, while the causality of infringement should have the property that "input A necessarily produces output B." Using the same generative model with the same instruction cannot generate the same infringing content: for example, inputting prompt A three times generates outputs B, C, and D respectively. Assuming that generating output B from prompt A constitutes infringement of work b, the result comparison method will find substantial similarity; however, generating outputs C and D will not constitute infringement of work b.

In such cases, neither the user nor the AI developer shall be liable for direct infringement. The user cannot guarantee that content generated using a specific prompt will necessarily infringe existing works, and the developer cannot predict or control AI output content, thus not constituting direct infringement—but may be liable for indirect infringement. The determination of direct and indirect infringement depends on factors such as who inputs the data (user or platform), whether the use is private and interactive, whether the platform uses the data to train models, and whether the platform provides dissemination services.

3.3.3 Restrictions on AIGC Rights: Application of Fair Use and Statutory Licensing

Fair Use: Unauthorized Use Permitted for Personal Learning and News Reporting.

Fair use refers to a legal act where, under specific conditions, the law allows others to freely use copyrighted works without obtaining the right holder's permission or paying remuneration—provided that such use does not affect the normal use of the work or unreasonably prejudice the legitimate interests of the copyright holder.

Article 24 of China's Copyright Law stipulates 13 scenarios of fair use, including:

Use for personal study, research, or appreciation;
Quoting others' works to illustrate a point;
Use in news reporting (e.g., publishing or broadcasting published current affairs articles or speeches delivered at public gatherings);
Use for classroom teaching or research;
Use for performing official duties;
Free public performances of others' works;
Translation of published works into ethnic minority languages;
Copying, photographing, or video recording artworks on public display.[27]

[27] "Fair Use" Under the Copyright Law. WeChat Official Account "Intellectual Sharing Perspective", March 30, 2023.

Collectively, these scenarios require fair use to be non-commercial and non-profit-oriented, serving the public interest. AIGC works are equally subject to these fair use provisions—for example, using AIGC for personal learning or news reporting does not require authorization.

Statutory Licensing: Applicable for Teaching and Scientific Research by Educational and Research Institutions.

Statutory licensing allows users to use published works without the copyright holder's permission but requires payment of reasonable remuneration, subject to statutory circumstances. China's Copyright Law specifies four types of statutory licensing and one quasi-statutory licensing:

Reprinting by newspapers and periodicals;
Producing sound recordings;
Broadcasting published works by radio or television stations;
Compiling and publishing textbooks;
Producing and providing courseware;
Quasi-statutory licensing: Providing specific works to rural areas through the internet.

Both fair use and statutory licensing are limited to legally prescribed scenarios, aiming to promote the circulation of information into the public domain by restricting copyright. The key difference is that statutory licensing requires payment of reasonable remuneration, while fair use imposes a more significant limitation on copyright by exempting remuneration obligations. AIGC works are also subject to these statutory licensing provisions—for example, educational and research institutions may use AIGC for teaching and scientific research under statutory licensing.

References

1. Qian W (2024) Third discussion on the position of AI-generated content in copyright law. Studies in Law and Business 3
2. Yiheng L, Zheng Z (2025) The construction of AIGC originality standards. Big Data Research 1:36–44
3. Shilin L, Cheng H (2025) Dilemmas and solutions for copyright infringement determination of AI-generated content. Cross-Strait Legal Science 5:15–27
4. Huibin Z, Huaibin W (2025) From Technicalism to legal evaluation: possibilities and judgment standards for copyright infringement by AIGC. Editorial Friend 11
5. Leval PN (1990) toward a fair use standard. Harv L Rev 103:1105

Chapter 4
Copyright Infringement Liability and Risk Prevention in the Application Process of Generative AI

In the scenario of generative AI, multiple liability subjects are involved, including model developers, platform operators, and end users. However, unlike the traditional binary infringement structure of "platform-user" on the internet, generative AI has formed a ternary infringement structure of "developer-operator-user". Therefore, in the liability chain of generative AI, accurately identifying liability subjects is a prerequisite for determining which laws to apply and how to apply them.

For developers, clarifying their liability scope in the entire generative AI ecosystem will drive them to prioritize compliant model development and legal data training. As the intermediate link connecting developers and users, operators play a bridging role in the generative AI scenario. Defining their status as liability subjects can urge them to actively fulfill their obligations of compliant operation. For example, in terms of content moderation, operators will invest more resources in establishing and improving content moderation mechanisms to fulfill their liability obligations. For users, clarifying their identity as liability subjects in generative AI can standardize their usage behaviors.

Therefore, this chapter focuses on the practical issues of generative AI—the division of liability subjects for copyright infringement, constitutive elements, as well as risk prevention and compliance measures for developers, operators, and users, addressing the practical needs of "who should be liable and how to avoid liability". This helps promote the healthy and innovative development of generative AI technology on the premise of safeguarding social and public interests, and avoids innovation suppression caused by unclear liability.

L. Cheng, *Copyright Issues Related to Generative Artificial Intelligence (AI)*, Artificial Intelligence and the Rule of Law,
https://doi.org/10.1007/978-981-95-8781-0_4

4.1 Division of Copyright Infringement Liability Subjects

In reality, the liability for copyright infringement of generative AI has become difficult to define. The core causes lie in three interwoven factors: algorithm black box at the technical level, overlapping roles of subjects in the industrial chain, and insufficient adaptation of existing legal rules. These three factors have greatly affected the division of copyright infringement liability subjects of generative AI, making it difficult to apply the identification logic of traditional tort liability.

At the technical level, the opacity of generative AI algorithms and the complexity of the generation process make it difficult to clarify the causal relationship between copyright infringement acts and damage consequences, and it is impossible to accurately locate the liability subjects of infringement as in traditional infringement scenarios. On one hand, the model training of generative AI relies on massive data and continuously optimizes through self-learning. Even developers cannot match the output content of generative AI with the original training data. Similarly, the algorithm black box will cause cognitive barriers. Operators often defend themselves on the grounds that they cannot predict the specific content generated by users using AI. In judicial practice, the subjective cognition of operators can only be presumed through indirect methods such as the composition analysis of training data, which indirectly confirms the technical difficulty of causal chain tracing.[1]

On the other hand, the output of generative AI is uncertain—different results may be generated under the same instruction, making the correlation between copyright infringement acts and consequences more ambiguous. For example, in the well-known Hangzhou "AI Ultraman" infringement case,[2] users of the involved AI platform could upload Ultraman materials to train the model, and after model superposition, they could stably generate similar images. However, the infringing materials were uploaded by users, and the release of the generated infringing content was also determined by users; the platform did not directly provide infringing works. At this time, it was difficult to define whether the infringement consequences were caused by the user's uploading behavior or the platform's failure to set up technical prevention and control mechanisms. The court had to analyze the stages of data input and content output one by one, and finally determined that the platform constituted contributory infringement, highlighting the obstacle of causal tracing at the technical level to liability definition.

At the industrial level, the industrial chain of generative AI includes multiple subjects such as model developers, data trainers, platform operators, end users, and disseminators, breaking the binary subject structure of traditional infringement. In some cases, some subjects may have overlapping roles—they may be both technology developers and service providers, leading to the inapplicability of existing

[1] Heqi [1].

[2] Civil Judgment (2024) Zhe 0192 Min Chu No. 1587, Hangzhou Internet Court; Civil Judgment (2024) Zhe 01 Min Zhong No. 10332, Hangzhou Intermediate People's Court.

standards for dividing liability subjects.[3] The blurring of role boundaries between different subjects, coupled with the limited liability borne by users, leads to the imbalance between rights and obligations. For example, in the aforementioned Hangzhou "AI Ultraman" case, the defendant platform had a dual identity as both a service provider and a disseminator of infringing content. The defendant claimed that it was only a service provider for information storage and should be exempt from liability under the "safe harbor" rule; while the plaintiff argued that the defendant had an attitude of allowing the spread of the generated infringing content and should bear infringement liability.

At the legal level, the characteristics of independent generation and self-optimization of generative AI conflict with the rule logic of traditional laws. Relevant laws and regulations are mostly principled provisions, lacking refined standards, resulting in no accurate basis for defining the liability subjects of infringement. The Interim Measures for the Administration of Generative Artificial Intelligence Services only makes general provisions on generative AI. The applicable standards of the "three-step test" for fair use are vague in the generative AI scenario. AI companies often claim fair use on the grounds that data training behavior belongs to "transformative use", but legal standards vary in different regions, making it even more impossible to have a unified basis for identifying the liability subjects of cross-border AI copyright infringement.

Similarly, the Interim Measures for the Administration of Generative Artificial Intelligence Services defines the liability of service providers as "producer liability", but AI provides services rather than products, and the application of product liability without fault is inconsistent with the logic of service liability with fault. Moreover, AI service providers cannot fully control the generated content, and the fault identification standard of "knowing or should have known" is difficult to define, making it difficult to implement the imputation principle in practice.[4]

It can be seen that generative AI has further strengthened the reproduction and dissemination of works, and at the same time led to the complexity of identifying the liability subjects of copyright infringement. As mentioned above, the value chain of the generative AI industry involves multiple subjects such as developers, operators, and users, among which:

Developers refer to individuals or organizations engaged in model development-related activities such as algorithm design, data collection and preprocessing, AI model training and verification, such as cloud computing service providers and open-source framework developers;

Operators refer to individuals or organizations that call models developed by others through programmable interfaces, integrate them into APPs or industrial processes, and then provide artificial intelligence services to the market;

Users refer to individuals or organizations that actually operate and use artificial intelligence systems in accordance with the service mode set by operators.

---

[3] Linghan and Lin [2].

[4] Jinliang [3].

In practice, the identities of developers and operators may overlap—for example, the development subject of a foundation model provides content generation services to users at the same time, or operators provide the model to users for use after training and optimizing it.[5] Therefore, it is necessary to clearly divide the liability subjects of copyright infringement of generative AI. Based on the three core division criteria of legal provisions, duty of care, and technical control ability, combined with regulations such as the Interim Measures for the Administration of Generative Artificial Intelligence Services and the case adjudication rules formed in judicial practice, it is possible to accurately define the three core subjects of developer-operator-user.

4.1.1 Developer Liability Scenarios and Exemption Circumstances

As core builders of generative AI, developers are responsible for model architecture design, training data screening, and model training. While broadly categorized as internet service providers, they essentially bear liability analogous to "content producers." Their copyright infringement liability primarily arises in three core links—training data, the model itself, and output content—with exemptions typically relying on copyright law rules such as fair use, legal authorization, and the technical neutrality defense.

Core Liability Scenarios

(1) Unauthorized Use of Copyrighted Content for Model Training

The most typical copyright infringement scenario in generative AI involves developers using copyrighted content to train models without authorization. When developers incorporate copyrighted text, images, videos, or other content into training datasets without the copyright holder's permission or statutory exemption, they may infringe upon rights such as the right of reproduction and the right of information network dissemination. While the model training phase itself does not generate infringement risks, the act of copying during data input and content reproduction during output may both fall within the scope of copyright control.[6]

For example:

In November 2025, the Munich Regional Court of Germany ruled that OpenAI had infringed copyright by using lyrics managed by Germany's music copyright collective management organization (GEMA) without authorization. GEMA accused OpenAI of using its copyrighted music library to train the ChatGPT model

---

[5] Hu and Ludi [4].

[6] Wenyi and Dongmei [5].

without permission or payment. Despite OpenAI's defense that it "learned content features rather than engaging in simple reproduction" and claimed exemption under text and data mining (TDM) rules, the court found that the lyrics were fully stored in the model's parameters and could be completely reproduced through simple prompts. This copying was not accidental and exceeded the scope of TDM exemptions, leading to a ruling that the model's memorization and reproduction of lyrics constituted copyright infringement and ordering OpenAI to pay compensation.

In a lawsuit filed by U.S. record labels against AI music generator Suno, Suno was accused of infringing the right of reproduction and information network dissemination by using copyrighted music works to train its AI music model. Unlike OpenAI's litigation defense, the parties resolved the dispute through cooperation—Suno abandoned the disputed model and launched a new one based on authorized content.

Thus, AI developers must complete copyright compliance reviews before data acquisition and training to avoid infringement risks.

(2) Infringement of AI Model Structure and Parameters

Another liability scenario occurs when developers plagiarize the core elements of others' original, copyright-protected AI models—such as model structure and training parameters—for their own model development or performance optimization. According to research by China Court Network, a model's structure and parameters together form its technical core: the structure determines the model's computing method and processing capabilities, while parameters dictate how the model generates outputs based on input data. Their combination directly reflects the developer's intellectual investment and commercial competitiveness.[7]

A landmark case illustrating this is the 2025 judgment by the Beijing Intellectual Property Court in Douyin v. B612 Kaji (China's first effective judgment explicitly protecting AI model structure and parameters). The plaintiff, Beijing Douyin Technology Co., Ltd., invested tens of millions of yuan and assembled a professional team (including over 20 hand-painters who created more than 50,000 original comics as training data) to develop its "Anime Transformation" AI filter. After nearly 10 months of model iteration, the filter attracted nearly 20 million users and formed a significant market competitive advantage. Two months after its launch, the defendant's app "B612 Kaji" released a highly similar "Shoujo Manga" filter. Technical comparison revealed that the core structural elements of the two models—including overall network structure, non-adjacent sub-network connections, and the number and position of convolutional layers—were identical. Among 36 convolutional layers, 33 had identical parameters (a similarity rate of 91.7%), and the generated effects were highly consistent in user-perceptible aspects such as lines, colors, and facial proportions. The court confirmed that AI model structure and parameters are protectable under the Anti-Unfair Competition Law, ordering

[7] Song Jianbao. Intellectual Property Protection for the Structure and Parameters of Artificial Intelligence Models. China Court Network, October 23, 2025. https://www.chinacourt.cn/article/detail/2025/10/id/9034555.shtml.

the defendant to cease infringement and compensate the plaintiff for economic losses and reasonable expenses totaling 1.6 million yuan. The second-instance judgment upheld the original ruling and became effective.[8]

When an AI model cannot obtain comprehensive protection under copyright law (e.g., parameter data does not constitute a work) or meet patent authorization standards, the Anti-Unfair Competition Law serves as an important protection pathway. Any act of plagiarizing to avoid R&D costs will incur legal liability.

(3) Output Content Infringement Due to Model Design Defects

Developers may also be liable if design flaws in the model lead to infringing output—specifically, failing to implement infringement prevention and filtering mechanisms during algorithm design, resulting in the model generating content substantially similar to copyrighted works. As controllers of model technology, developers are obligated to anticipate and prevent infringement risks arising from algorithmic defects. This obligation does not require direct control over generated content but rather a duty of care derived from their technical dominance. Scholars argue that liability for generative AI—characterized by a mix of "black box" and "gray box" technologies—should focus on risk prediction and prevention measures during the design phase.[9]

In Getty Images v. Stability AI, Getty Images accused Stability AI of using 12 million of its copyrighted images to train the Stable Diffusion model without authorization. Critically, the defendant failed to implement any verification, filtering, or avoidance mechanisms for copyrighted materials in its algorithm design—neither screening infringing content in training data through vector comparison technology nor embedding algorithms to block "substantially similar" content during generation, resulting in inherent design flaws. While no effective judgment on copyright infringement was issued, the case conveyed a key judicial stance: developers bear a high duty of care regarding the legality of training data and algorithmic infringement risks. Where output content can be traced to specific copyrighted works, such design flaws will serve as core evidence for finding fault.

Exemption Circumstances

Developers may be exempt from liability in three primary scenarios: qualifying for fair use under copyright law, fulfilling a reasonable duty of care, and possessing complete authorization proof for lawfully sourced data.

(1) Fair Use for Non-Commercial Scientific Research Purposes

[8] Liu Shan. "Anime Transformation Filter" Infringement Case Concluded on Appeal—AI Model Structure and Parameters Cannot Be Used Arbitrarily. China Intellectual Property News Network, October 16, 2025. http://www.iprchn.com/cipnews/news_content.aspx?newsId=144096.

[9] Chengjie [6].

Developers may claim exemption under fair use if model training is conducted for non-commercial scientific research, provided the use does not interfere with the normal exploitation of the work or unreasonably prejudice the copyright holder's legitimate interests. The four-factor test under Section 107 of the U.S. Copyright Act provides a normative framework for determining fair use in AI training scenarios. Scholars note that this framework offers actionable judicial standards for fair use defenses in AI training, with "non-commercial nature" and "no substitutive impact on the market" being key factors for exemption in infringement cases.[10]

Landmark cases illustrating this standard include:

Bartz v. Anthropic (U.S., 2025): The court ruled that Anthropic's use of lawfully acquired books to train large language models (LLMs) for algorithm optimization constituted fair use. The model was not used for commercial services, and the generated content had no direct connection to the original works.[11] This case demonstrates that AI training is more likely to satisfy fair use when it serves algorithmic innovation rather than commercial competition.

Thomson Reuters v. Ross Intelligence (U.S., 2025): The defendant claimed fair use on the grounds that "model training constitutes technical research," but the court found the model was directly used for commercial financial data analysis services, competing with the plaintiff's core business, and thus rejected the defense.[12]

Notably, non-commercial scientific research is not an absolute exemption. Developers must still satisfy requirements such as "not affecting the normal use of the work" and "not prejudicing the copyright holder's legitimate interests." Even for research purposes, "excessive use" or "potential market substitution" may exceed the boundaries of fair use, providing clear compliance guidance for developers.

(2) Fulfillment of Reasonable Duty of Care

Developers may be exempt if they have implemented necessary infringement prevention measures for the model and promptly addressed infringement after receiving notices, with the actual infringement caused by user operations. Due to the black box nature of generative AI algorithms and user autonomy, developers cannot achieve absolute control over all generated results. They should not be held liable beyond their technical capabilities; instead, liability should focus on whether they have fulfilled a reasonable duty of care commensurate with their technical level. For example, if a developer optimizes keyword filtering and restricts training on well-known IPs after being found liable for infringing output, and a user later

[10] Wang Fei, He Menglin, Pu Kejie. Sorting Out the Application of Fair Use Rules Through Global AIGC Training Data Infringement Lawsuits. Zhonglun Law Firm Official Website, December 24, 2024. https://www.zhonglun.com/research/articles/53915.html.

[11] Bartz et al. v. Anthropic PBC, Civil Judgment (2025) 3:23-cv-03417-vc, United States District Court for the Northern District of California. https://storage.courtlistener.com/recap/gov.uscourts.cand.434709/gov.uscourts.cand.434709.231.0_2.pdf.

[12] Thomson Reuters Enterprise Centre GmbH v. Ross Intelligence Inc., Civil Judgment (2025) 1:20-cv-613-SB, United States District Court for the District of Delaware. https://www.ded.uscourts.gov/sites/ded/files/opinions/20-613_5.pdf.

modifies materials to maliciously bypass these measures, the developer may claim exemption by proving fulfillment of its reasonable review obligation.[13]

(3) Complete Copyright Authorization Proof

Developers are exempt if they can provide complete copyright authorization documents, proving that all training data is legally authorized and the training activity has obtained the copyright holder's consent. For instance, in the aforementioned Suno compliance transformation case, after collaborating with record labels, Suno adopted authorized music works as training data. Subsequent models trained on this authorized dataset avoided copyright disputes due to lawful data sourcing. This model of "legal authorization + profit sharing" has become a typical compliance pathway for developers to avoid copyright infringement.

The EU's Copyright in the Digital Single Market Directive provides an alternative compliance option beyond authorization by establishing TDM exception rules. Articles 4(1) and 4(2) legalize TDM in general scenarios, allowing any entity to reproduce or extract data from lawfully acquired content for TDM purposes—providing a compliance basis for AI developers to use such content for model training. Articles 4(3) and 3(3) explicitly recognize the copyright holder's right to reserve rights: if the holder makes a reasonable and clear reservation, developers may not use the corresponding content for TDM or model training without authorization; conversely, using content without such a reservation does not constitute infringement. In practice, the Directive reduces developers' authorization costs (public works without rights reservation can be directly used for training) while safeguarding the copyright holder's right to autonomous decision-making through the rights reservation clause. Developers can thus choose an appropriate pathway based on their specific scenarios, avoiding training data infringement risks through complete authorization proof or precise application of statutory exception rules.

4.1.2 Operator Liability Scenarios and Exemption Circumstances

Unlike developers, generative AI operators focus on providing AI services to end users. Their copyright infringement liability primarily arises from facilitating user infringement or failing to control infringing output, while exemptions rely on fulfilling statutory obligations, transformative use, and lack of causal connection to infringement.

13 Bingyin [7].

Core Liability Scenarios

(1) Facilitating User Infringement Through Service Design or Lack of Control

Operators may be liable for contributory infringement if they offer model training functions targeting specific copyrighted works and fail to review or remove infringing models or generated content widely disseminated on their platforms. Even without participating in underlying model design, their service design and inadequate oversight become key factors in the spread of infringement.

A typical example is the aforementioned Hangzhou "AI Ultraman" case: the defendant, as an AI platform operator, allowed users to train and share Ultraman AI models, leading to the generation of content substantially similar to the copyrighted Ultraman images. Article 15 of the Interim Measures for the Administration of Generative Artificial Intelligence Services requires providers to "establish and improve complaint and reporting mechanisms, set up convenient entry points, publish processing procedures and feedback time limits, and promptly accept, handle, and respond to public complaints and reports." Based on this provision, the court found the defendant liable for failing to implement complaint/reporting mechanisms or infringement risk prompts, ordering it to cease infringement and compensate for losses.

(2) Active Promotion of Infringing Content

Operators may infringe the right of information network dissemination if they actively recommend, pin, or prominently display infringing content posted by users, expanding its reach beyond mere technical service provision. In the "AI Ultraman" case, infringing works generated by user-trained models were featured on the platform's homepage and other prominent sections. Article 7 of the Interpretation of the Supreme People's Court on Several Issues Concerning the Application of Law in the Trial of Civil Disputes Involving Infringement of the Right of Information Network Dissemination stipulates that network service providers are liable for contributory infringement if they "know or should know that network users are infringing the right of information network dissemination through their services but fail to take necessary measures such as deletion, blocking, or disconnection of links, or provide technical support." The court held that the defendant, as a platform operator, failed to fulfill a reasonable duty of care regarding infringing content involving a high-profile IP and did not implement necessary prevention and control measures, ultimately finding it liable for infringing the right of information network dissemination.

(3) Failing to Control Infringing Output or Fulfill Labeling Obligations

Operators may be liable if their services generate content substantially similar to copyrighted works in response to user prompts, without implementing filtering mechanisms or fulfilling labeling obligations. In The New York Times v. OpenAI, The New York Times accused ChatGPT (operated by OpenAI) and Microsoft's Bing Chat of generating content highly overlapping with its news reports and falsely attributing misinformation to the newspaper. Based on Section 106 of the U.S. Copyright Act, which protects core rights such as reproduction and distribution, the court recognized the reasonableness of the plaintiff's numerous infringement examples and held OpenAI, as the service operator, accountable for the dispute.[14]

(4) Providing Customized Services Without Instruction Review

Operators offering customized generation services (e.g., custom paintings, copywriting, or videos) may be liable if they fail to review user instructions requesting infringing content, leading to direct output of infringing works. In a landmark 2023 lawsuit, visual artists including Anderson sued Midjourney, Stability AI, and DeviantArt, accusing them of scraping 5 billion copyrighted images (including their own works) to train AI painting tools without authorization. While the court dismissed the direct infringement claims due to insufficient evidence of the defendants' participation in training, the case clarified that AI service operators face liability risks if they provide channels for customized infringement. It also prompted industry adjustments, such as Stability AI introducing a mechanism allowing artists to opt out of having their works used to train future versions of Stable Diffusion.

Exemption Circumstances

Operators' exemptions differ from developers' due to their focus on public service provision, content distribution, and platform management. Key exemptions include:

(1) Fulfilling the "Notice-and-Takedown" Obligation and Reasonable Duty of Care

Operators may invoke the "safe harbor" rule for network service providers if they merely offer technical services, do not participate in user infringement, and promptly take necessary measures to stop infringement upon receiving notices—distinct from developers' direct liability for training data legality.

A landmark Chinese case is the 2025 "Medusa" case (Shanghai's first substantive judgment on AI model copyright): the plaintiff, copyright holder of the "Medusa" character from the Fights Break Sphere anime series, sued a user (Li) and an AI image generation platform. Li had created two "Medusa" LoRA models (a lightweight fine-tuning technology) using 20+ screenshots of the character and made them available on the platform, enabling other users to generate substantially similar images. The platform argued that LoRA technology is neutral and non-infringing, and it had promptly taken down the models, notified overseas partners, and fulfilled the statutory "notice-and-takedown" obligation upon receiving the lawsuit. The court ruled the platform not liable, finding it did not participate in material

[14] New York Court Rules in Favor of News Organizations in OpenAI Infringement Case. China Intellectual Property Protection Network, April 17, 2025. http://ipr.mofcom.gov.cn/article/gjxw/gbhj/bmz/mg/202504/1991202.html.

extraction, training, or publication of the models, and had implemented complaint/reporting and review mechanisms, acting without fault.[15]

(2) Providing Transformative Services Qualifying for Fair Use

Operators may claim exemption if their use of copyrighted works is transformative—creating new functions or expressions through technical means rather than simple reproduction. In Kadrey et al. v. Meta (2025), authors accused Meta of using pirated books to train its LLaMA model. Meta argued fair use, emphasizing the model's transformative purpose (developing language tools for translation and summarization) and lack of direct dissemination of original content or substantial market substitution. The court ruled Meta's use qualified as fair use, exempting it from liability.[16]

Scholars note that generative AI typically does not "memorize" training data, and its output often involves fragmented recombination. If operators' services only assist in creative conception (transformative use) rather than reproducing original works, they may claim fair use under the Copyright Law.[17] Professor Hu Kaizhong adds that general-purpose AI services have minimal reliance on individual copyrighted works, rarely constituting substantial similarity—this low-density use aligns with core fair use characteristics, distinguishing it from high-risk targeted training and warranting appropriate exemption space for operators.[18]

(3) No Causal Connection Between Services and Infringement

Operators may be exempt if infringement is independently committed by a third party, and there is no evidence of the operator abetting, assisting, or participating in the act, or of a causal link between its services and the infringement. For example, in Getty Images v. Stability AI, Stability AI argued that model training was independently conducted by developers, and as a service operator, it only provided external use interfaces without participating in data scraping or training—lacking a causal connection to infringement. In the absence of evidence of joint infringement intent between the operator, developer, and user, liability may be reduced or exempted.

(4) Strict Compliance with Regulatory Norms and Labeling Obligations

Operators may be exempt if they strictly adhere to regulations such as the Interim Measures for the Administration of Generative Artificial Intelligence Services, the Measures for the Labeling of AI-Generated Synthetic Content, and the Regulations on the Administration of Deep Synthesis Internet Information Services—fulfilling

---

[15] User Fines 50,000 Yuan for Feeding "Medusa" Character to AI Model to Generate Images. Southern Metropolis Daily, November 5, 2025. https://www.toutiao.com/article/7569237222700958244/?channel=&source=search_tab.

[16] Meta Achieves "Mixed Results" in AI "Piracy" Lawsuit. China Intellectual Property Protection Network, August 11, 2025. https://ipr.mofcom.gov.cn/article/gjxw/gbhj/bmz/mg/202507/1992561.html.

[17] Bingyin [7].

[18] Kaizhong and Ludi [8], pp. 44–53.

obligations such as labeling AI-generated content and setting infringement risk prompts. While these regulations do not explicitly state "compliance equals exemption," they provide clear standards for operators, serving as core evidence of lack of fault in judicial practice.

Article 7 of the Interim Measures requires providers to "lawfully conduct training data processing activities such as pre-training and fine-tuning."

Article 15 mandates complaint/reporting mechanisms.

The Labeling Measures specify explicit and implicit labeling scenarios.

Article 17 of the Deep Synthesis Regulations requires prominent labeling of content likely to cause public confusion.

Fulfilling these service-side risk control and disclosure obligations establishes a legal basis for fault exemption, distinct from developers' data-side compliance duties.[19]

4.1.3 User Liability Scenarios and Exemption Circumstances

As direct manipulators of generative AI tools, users' copyright infringement primarily occurs in independent operation links—such as selecting specific infringing materials, disseminating AI-generated infringing content, or secondary processing leading to substantial similarity with others' works. This is fundamentally distinct from developers' responsibilities for model design and data training, and operators' obligations for platform supervision.

Core Liability Scenarios

(1) Targeted Feeding of Infringing Materials

To meet specific generation needs, users may actively select unauthorized copyrighted works as targeted training materials for AI models or upload them to AI platforms to assist content generation. This act directly infringes the copyright holder's right of reproduction; if the model or content generated from such materials is made public, it may also infringe the right of information network dissemination.

A typical example is the aforementioned Shanghai "Medusa" AI model infringement case: User Li arbitrarily intercepted over 20 images of the "Medusa" character from the Fights Break Sphere anime, used the AI platform's LoRA fine-tuning function to generate a customized model, and publicly released it on the platform for others to use. The court found that Li's commercial-purpose conduct met the "substantial similarity" standard for copyright infringement, violating the copyright holder's right of reproduction and information network dissemination, and ultimately ordered him to compensate for economic losses.

---

[19] Jianfeng [9].

(2) Commercial Use of Infringing Generated Content

Users may infringe upon proprietary rights such as the right of distribution and information network dissemination by using AI to generate content substantially similar to others' copyrighted works (or directly containing others' copyrighted elements) and using it for commercial activities (e.g., advertising, paid licensing) without the copyright holder's permission.

For instance, in a case where a Beijing company used AI to counterfeit host Li Zimeng's image for commercial live streaming,[20] the defendant company operated a video account with hundreds of thousands of followers. To promote its fish oil products, the company's employees collected news clips of well-known CCTV host Li Zimeng, edited and synthesized fake recommendation videos using AI technology. The fake Li Zimeng in the videos claimed the fish oil had medical effects such as treating dizziness, headaches, and memory loss. Sold at 59.9 yuan for three bottles, the product showed 177,000 units sold. Investigations revealed the fish oil was merely ordinary candy with no medical efficacy. The company's unauthorized use of Li Zimeng's image for commercial live streaming via AI infringed her right of portrait, consumers' right to know, and potentially the copyright of the original video creators.

(3) Infringing "Mashups" of Classic Works

Users may infringe the copyright holder's right of adaptation by using AI to drastically modify classic copyrighted works (e.g., films, literature)—distorting plots, altering character settings, and disseminating the modified content. For example, users might use AI tools to "mash up" classic works like Legend of Zhen Huan or Journey to the West—converting Legend of Zhen Huan into a Studio Ghibli-style animation for online dissemination, or adapting Lin Daiyu into an absurd "willow-tree-lifting" character in profit-making short videos. Such acts, if exceeding the scope of satire or parody and substituting the original work's views or damaging its market value, infringe the original author's right of information network dissemination and adaptation.[21]

Notably, these "mashup" acts are not for personal enjoyment or developers' technical testing but deliberate attempts to pursue dissemination effects and commercial interests. Similarly, in generative AI scenarios, some users may use AI models to learn the story frameworks and character settings of novels, generate "sequels" or "adaptations," and sell them on e-commerce platforms. These user-generated counterfeit works directly compete with the original works in the market, infringing the original author's right of adaptation and distribution.

(4) Infringement in Assisted Creation

---

[20] CCTV Host's AI Counterfeit Used for Live Streaming: Official Announcement. Legal Network, October 16, 2025. https://www.toutiao.com/article/7561643452724511258/?&source=m_redirect.

[21] Zhao Li. AI "Mashups": Creative Freedom or Infringement? Legal Daily·Rule of Law Perspective, April 26, 2025.

When using generative AI as an auxiliary creation tool, users may be liable for copyright infringement if they fail to fulfill a reasonable legality review obligation—directly adopting AI-generated content containing the core original expressions of others' copyrighted works, or integrating/adapting such infringing content into their own works for public release. The core of this liability lies in users' "review obligation" and "fault liability": AI itself does not generate infringement, but users have dominant control over the selection and use of AI-generated content. Failure to perform necessary verification obligations makes them liable for infringing consequences.

Exemption Circumstances

Users' exemptions focus on the legality and faultlessness of their own use, differing significantly from developers' reliance on duty of care or operators' reliance on the "safe harbor" rule. Key exemptions include:

(1) Legally Authorized Use of AI-Generated Content

Article 4 of the Interim Measures for the Administration of Generative Artificial Intelligence Services requires respecting intellectual property and commercial ethics, prohibiting monopolistic or unfair competitive acts. Legal authorization is a primary compliance pathway. If users have obtained explicit authorization from the copyright holder to use AI for assisted creation or secondary processing of authorized content, they are exempt from liability even if the generated content is related to the original work. This differs from developers' infringement risks of scraping unauthorized data for model training.

(2) Non-Commercial Assisted Creation Qualifying for Fair Use

Users may claim exemption if their AI-assisted creation meets the requirements of fair use under the Copyright Law—e.g., for non-commercial purposes such as personal study, research, or commentary—without prejudicing the copyright holder's legitimate interests. Fair use encourages new forms of expression that do not substitute the original work's market. Unlike developers' large-scale scraping of data for commercial model training, users' fair use is typically small-scale and non-profit.

(3) Unknowing Infringement Due to Operator/Developer Fault

Users may be exempt from liability if they generate infringing content through normal operations without knowledge or fault, caused by operators' failure to review output content or developers' model defects. Liability in such cases usually falls on negligent operators or developers with technical flaws, but users' exemption hinges on the absence of active infringing intent. Scholars argue that user liability should depend on whether they actively engaged in acts like material interception or targeted training; passive use of defective platform models without subjective malice should not constitute infringement, aligning with the fault liability principle in the Civil Code.

(4) No "Substantial Similarity" to Original Copyrighted Works

Users may claim exemption if they only input broad prompts (not targeting specific copyrighted works) and the generated content has no substantial similarity to others' copyrighted works—even if there is occasional partial overlap. The core defense lies in the independence of creation and non-similarity of content. Courts focus on whether AI output constitutes substantial reproduction or counterfeiting of copyrighted works; absence of this feature exempts users from liability regardless of the AI model's training process.

4.2 Constitutive Elements and Forms of Copyright Infringement Liability

4.2.1 Constitutive Elements of Copyright Infringement Liability

(1) Infringing Act

Unlike general infringement, generative AI copyright infringement exhibits a full-chain distribution feature, and the nature of the act must be defined in conjunction with technical principles.

Training Data Infringement: Unauthorized reproduction or transmission of copyrighted works into training datasets, infringing the copyright holder's right of reproduction and right of information network dissemination. Large-scale copying of protected works for training is currently the most typical infringing act—for example, in the aforementioned "GEMA v. OpenAI" and "Getty Images v. Stability AI" cases, defendants were accused of infringing the original copyright holders' right of reproduction.

Model Infringement: Plagiarizing the original structure and core parameters of others' AI models. In the "Douyin Anime Transformation Filter v. B612 Kaji Shoujo Manga Filter" case, the defendant's model's network structure and convolutional layer parameters were highly similar to the plaintiff's, constituting an infringement of competitive interests under the Anti-Unfair Competition Law.

Output Content Infringement: Generation of content substantially similar to copyrighted works due to model design defects or user operations, infringing the copyright holder's right of reproduction, distribution, etc.

Secondary Use Infringement of AI-Generated Content: Unauthorized reproduction, adaptation, or attribution of AI-generated content without the permission of its right holder (e.g., removing watermarks from AI-generated works for commercial use, or arbitrarily disseminating copyrighted AI images as illustrations). In China's first "AI text-to-image" copyright case, the plaintiff Li generated images by inputting prompts and adjusting parameters; the court recognized his intellectual input as originality, granting him copyright. The defendant Liu's unauthorized use of the images with watermarks removed constituted infringement of the right of attribution and information network dissemination.[22]

Memorization-Based Invisible Infringement: Models store the core expressions of works due to "memorization effects," enabling users to obtain content highly consistent with the original works through simple prompts. This reproduction stems from deliberate storage rather than AI's learning optimization.

(2) Harmful Consequences

Harmful consequences of generative AI copyright infringement primarily affect copyright holders' rights and public interests, with diverse manifestations as AI application scenarios expand:

Property Damage: Direct reduction in licensing revenue and displacement of market share.

Moral Right Damage: AI's memorization-based reproduction of works often removes watermarks or attribution information, infringing the copyright holder's right of attribution and right of integrity.

Personality Interest Damage: Low-quality AI-generated works (e.g., exaggerated or distorted adaptations of classic works) may mislead the public about the original author's creative standards, harming their reputation.

Public Interest Damage: Uncompensated use of creators' works for AI training undermines their enthusiasm, conflicting with the legislative purpose of copyright law and weakening the innovation incentive mechanism, while disrupting the fair competitive order of the digital copyright market.

(3) Causal Relationship

Unlike the direct "one cause, one effect" relationship in traditional infringement, generative AI copyright infringement involves a "multi-subject, multi-link" causal chain due to technical intervention:

Direct Causal Relationship: For example, Stability AI's use of unauthorized images for training (act) → model generation of similar images (result) → Getty Images' commercial losses (harm). The infringing act is directly linked to the harm.

Indirect Causal Relationship: In the Hangzhou "AI Ultraman" case, the platform's failure to implement a well-known IP filtering mechanism (act) → users' generation of infringing images (result) → the plaintiff's intellectual property damage (harm). The court found an indirect causal relationship between the platform's failure to fulfill its review obligation and the harm.

Causal relationship in generative AI copyright infringement can be established through technical traceability—restoring the connection between acts and harm using evidence such as model parameters, training data logs, and generated content features.

(4) Fault Determination

---

[22] Li v. Liu, Copyright Infringement Dispute, Civil Judgment (2023) Jing 0491 Min Chu No. 11279, Beijing Internet Court, November 27, 2023.

The unified fault standard for traditional infringement is incompatible with generative AI's diverse liability subjects, as their control over technology and risk prevention obligations vary substantially. A gradient fault determination approach is therefore adopted, dividing liability boundaries based on subjects' control over AI technology and the intensity of their duty of care to achieve a match between rights and responsibilities:

Developers' Fault: Developers exercise absolute control over generative AI through model design and data training, requiring stricter fault standards. Fault includes intentional infringement (e.g., malicious plagiarism of model structures/parameters, large-scale illegal use of copyrighted data for training) and negligent infringement (e.g., lack of copyright review, model design defects).

Operators' Fault: Operators are primarily responsible for content distribution and user management, with weaker technical control than developers. Fault is presumed under the "know or should have known" standard—for example, deliberate disregard of infringing content or delayed response to infringement notices.

Users' Fault: As direct users of generative AI, users have no control over model development or training data. Fault determination focuses on malicious acts, such as deliberately bypassing platform/developer prevention measures or intentionally disseminating/adapting AI-generated infringing content with full knowledge of the infringement.

4.2.2 Forms of Generative AI Copyright Infringement Liability

(1) Cessation of Infringement

The most fundamental liability form, aiming to terminate infringing acts at the source and prevent further harm. It includes deleting infringing training data, removing AI-generated infringing content, disabling defective models, and shutting down illegally used AI service interfaces. Given generative AI's technical characteristics, simple cessation is often insufficient—extended obligations such as compliance rectification and technical remediation are required to form a complete liability chain. For example, an online medical platform that adapted a general AI model for diagnosis without optimizing special case recognition (resulting in infringing diagnostic recommendations) was ordered by regulators to supplement medical data for model training, add professional physician review procedures, and pass third-party safety assessments before re-launching.

(2) Compensation for Losses

The core liability form, generally applying the calculation logic of "actual loss first → infringer's profit as supplement → statutory compensation as fallback," with punitive damages available for malicious infringement.

Actual Loss: Determined with reference to copyright licensing fees, lost market share, etc.

Infringer's Profit: Calculated based on economic benefits obtained through infringement—for example, in the Changsha AI "one-click video production" case, the court awarded 800,000 yuan in compensation based on the defendant's membership fee revenue from infringement.[23]

Statutory Compensation: Determined comprehensively based on infringement circumstances, work value, and dissemination scope when actual loss or infringer's profit is difficult to calculate.

Scholars note that punitive damages may apply if evidence proves developers/operators deliberately tolerated infringement, combined with the scale of infringement.[24]

(3) Apology

Applicable only for infringement of copyright holders' moral rights (e.g., right of attribution, right of integrity) or natural persons' personality rights (e.g., portrait right, voice right), with strict scope limitations—excluding pure property right infringement. For example, AI models that strip attribution information when reproducing works or distort core expressions require an apology to the copyright holder; unauthorized use of others' portraits/voices to generate defamatory content via generative AI also requires an apology, with the form of performance matching the scope of infringement (e.g., publishing an apology on the platform where the infringement occurred).

(4) Elimination of Impact

Designed to remedy adverse effects on the right holder's reputation, work value, or industry ecology. For example, the infringing party may issue a statement clarifying the infringement on the homepage of its operating platform or authoritative industry media. In a case where an AI writing tool provided fake "grass-planting copy" for a social platform (disrupting the authentic content ecosystem), the court ordered the developer to publish a statement in industry media to eliminate impact.[25] In an AI portrait defamation case, the defendant was ordered to issue a statement in the WeChat group where defamatory images were posted to repair the plaintiff's reputation.[26]

---

[23] Tencent Technology et al. v. Beijing Baidu Netcom Technology et al., Copyright Infringement and Unfair Competition Dispute, Civil Judgment (2024) Xiang 01 Min Zhong No. 18114, Changsha Intermediate People's Court.

[24] Zhang Wurui. Research on the Application of Punitive Damages for Intellectual Property Infringement in Generative AI Scenarios. Zhiren Law Firm, December 5, 2025.

[25] Hangzhou Intermediate People's Court. Is AI-Generated "Grass-Planting Notes" a Normal Commercial Act or Unfair Competition? China Chang'an Network, September 12, 2025.

[26] Zhang v. Zhao, Portrait Right and Reputation Right Infringement Dispute, Civil Judgment (2024) Jing 0108 Min Chu No. 23456, Haidian District People's Court, October 15, 2024.

4.2.3 *Liability for Joint Infringement*

Generative AI copyright joint infringement involves multiple subjects (developers, operators, users), with liability based on fault liability. Joint and several liability or proportional liability is assigned according to subjective intent, role in the infringement chain, and control over technology:

Joint and Several Liability: Applies when multiple subjects have common infringing intent, jointly commit infringing acts, and cause the same harm. In Beijing Tongzhou District Court's first criminal case of AI-related copyright infringement, Luo and Yao conspired to instruct AI artists to fine-tune copyrighted artworks for puzzle production and sales; Li and Wang, as partners of Yao's e-commerce store, were responsible for customer service and complaint handling. With clear criminal intent and joint participation in the full chain of infringement (generation, production, sales), they constituted joint infringement, with each subject liable for the entire harm.[27]

Proportional Liability: Applies when multiple subjects have no common intent, but their independent acts indirectly combine to cause infringement, and the degree of fault and influence of each act can be clarified. For example, a developer's failure to filter infringing training data, an operator's lack of infringement prevention mechanisms, and a user's input of infringement-oriented prompts—all independently contributing to infringing content generation. Liability is allocated based on technical contribution, fault degree, and profit obtained.

4.3 Prevention Measures for Copyright Infringement Risks of Generative AI

With the rapid development of digital technology and the digital economy, copyright infringement incidents involving generative AI are on the rise. The core causes stem from multiple factors: the concealment of infringement due to technical characteristics, the lag of legal rules, the lack of industry compliance mechanisms, and the drastic reduction in creative thresholds.

First, at the technical level, AI model features make infringement more concealed. Currently, most training data rarely obtains explicit authorization from copyright holders, and developers often illegally crawl and use copyrighted texts, images, and other works under the pretext of "fair use." Meanwhile, the black box nature of AI models makes it difficult for original creators to trace whether their works have been included in training data—even if infringement is suspected, evidence collection is challenging. More critically, generative AI infringement is not

[27] Fuzhou XX E-Commerce Co., Ltd. et al. v. Luo et al., Copyright Infringement Case, Criminal Judgment, Tongzhou District People's Court, June 13, 2025, published in Criminal Trial Reference, Vol. 144 (No. 1658).

traditional direct copying but a "vague reproduction" of a work's style, core plot, and core expression. This non-direct form of infringement differs from the "access + substantial similarity" framework in copyright law, plunging judicial determination into a dilemma.

Second, at the legal level, rule lag and inadequate adaptability of the liability determination system persist. There is intense controversy over whether model training qualifies for fair use. This legal gap leaves many enterprises teetering on the edge of infringement. Additionally, the generative AI industrial chain involves multiple subjects (developers, operators, users), further extending the infringement liability chain. Judicial practice includes both rulings finding service providers liable for "direct infringement" and cases of "contributory infringement." This ambiguity in liability determination leads some subjects to take chances and neglect copyright compliance obligations.[28]

Third, at the practical level, high compliance costs and the absence of authorization mechanisms pose obstacles. For many enterprises, compliant data collection and training require substantial investment; for individuals, the cost of enforcing rights may far exceed potential benefits. Moreover, there is currently no efficient copyright authorization model adapted to AI creation—traditional models, designed primarily for human creation, cannot meet AI's demand for training on massive works.

Fourth, at the application level, the popularization of universal creation has fueled the spread of infringement. Generative AI has lowered the creative threshold, enabling "everyone to create," but the creative ability and copyright awareness of massive users vary widely. To pursue efficiency, many users arbitrarily use AI-generated content protected by others' copyrights for commercial promotion, paid publication, and other scenarios, ultimately leading to frequent copyright infringements.

Therefore, it is necessary to provide actionable compliance measures for different industries from the perspectives of various subjects, combined with their corresponding duties of care.

4.3.1 Developers

(1) Establish a Copyright Review Mechanism for Training Data and Mitigate Risks Through Classification Management

For example, Anthropic, the overseas AI enterprise behind the Claude large model, established a rigorous copyright review and classification mechanism for training data following a copyright lawsuit over its use of pirated books for training. On one hand, the company explicitly classifies training data into "legally purchased data" and "pirated data": millions of books legally bought from secondhand bookstores

[28] Hu and Ludi [4].

and distributors are scanned for model training, a practice deemed fair use by courts. On the other hand, approximately seven million books downloaded from pirated websites are not only excluded from training but also completely deleted and no longer stored.

China's ByteDance, in developing AI models such as Doubao, built a targeted data classification and review system. It divides training data into "verifiable data" (e.g., math problems, code) and "non-verifiable data" (e.g., creative writing). For verifiable data, a million-level triple cleaning process is implemented—manual screening, model filtering, and multi-model verification—retaining only high-value compliant data. For non-verifiable data, low-value and unknown-source samples are removed, and content quality is optimized through a pairwise comparison reward method. This classification review mechanism ensures data legality while adapting to the training needs of different content types, supporting the compliance of the Doubao model.[29]

Similarly, Apple emphasizes that it does not use any illegally obtained online data for AI model training. If publishers explicitly refuse to allow their content to be used for training, Apple will not crawl such data. It also clarifies that user private information or interaction data is not involved in foundation model training, and filtering mechanisms have been deployed to eliminate personally identifiable information and inappropriate content.[30]

(2) Purchase "Copyright-Clean Data" and Obtain Authorized Data from Legitimate Providers

In the image generation field, Bria—a company focused on compliant AI image generation—proactively collaborated with approximately 20 institutions (including Getty Images) to purchase authorized image data for model training, fully resolving copyright disputes over training data. Its foundation model includes 1 billion compliant visual assets and millions of video clips. Additionally, Bria calculates and automatically distributes compensation based on the "influence" of image owners on the dataset, ensuring copyright compliance while building a sound IP cooperation ecosystem.[31]

Google DeepMind, while not directly purchasing external copyright-clean data, converts legally sourced basic data into compliant training data through its unique "Generative Data Refinement (GDR)" technology. Using open-source code repositories, legally public web content, and other raw materials, the technology rewrites data via models to remove privacy information and infringement-risk content, generating refined datasets with both knowledge value and compliance. For example, in code data processing, sensitive information such as APIs (Application Programming

[29] ByteDance Discloses Technical Details of New Model Seed-Thinking-v1.5, API to Open on April 17. Sina Finance, April 14, 2025. https://finance.sina.com.cn/tech/digi/2025-04-15/doc-inetccsw9499783.shtml.

[30] Applebot Model Training and Individual Privacy Rights. Apple Official Website, July 23, 2025. https://support.apple.com/en-us/120320.

[31] Bria's Safety Architecture. Bria Official Website. https://bria.ai/brias-safety-architecture.

Interfaces) and Tokens are accurately replaced. APIs act as intermediaries defining interactions between software applications, allowing developers to leverage existing functions without writing code from scratch. Tokens are basic units converting natural language into model-processable form (words, punctuation, phrases), critical to model performance and resource needs. This process retains the training value of code while avoiding copyright or privacy issues from flawed data—essentially creating "copyright-clean data" through technical means, based on legitimate raw data.[32]

(3) Sign Data Authorization Agreements and Clarify Copyright Guarantee Liabilities of Providers

Some views hold that AI training data licensing contracts must establish a compliance system of "right cleanliness—use restrictions—derivative rights," where "right cleanliness" corresponds to the copyright guarantee liability of data providers, with composite cleanliness certification. Article 7 of the Interim Measures for the Administration of Generative Artificial Intelligence Services requires contracts to ensure: ① Copyright authorization (complying with the originality standard in Article 12 of the Copyright Law); ② Legal processing of personal information (in line with Article 13 of the Personal Information Protection Law); ③ Compliant data collection (meeting the explicit consent requirement in Article 41 of the Cybersecurity Law). The lack of such guarantees triggers the right to terminate the contract under Article 566 of the Civil Code. This provides a legal basis for designing copyright guarantee clauses in data authorization agreements and confirms their industry necessity.[33]

(4) Design Infringing Content Filtering Tools and Embed Review/Labeling Mechanisms

Microsoft has equipped its Azure AI-related generative tools with a core infringement-filtering tool—the "Protected Material Detection Filter"—divided into text and code modules. The text module scans for copyrighted content (e.g., song lyrics, article excerpts, recipes), while the code module targets protected code (e.g., proprietary source code, algorithms in GitHub repositories). When embedded into the content generation workflow, the tool automatically reviews content before delivery to users. If a high match with protected materials is detected, the content is immediately flagged, triggering actions such as blocking publication or requiring revisions.[34]

---

[32] Generative Data Refinement: Just Ask for Better Data. arXiv, September 11, 2025. https://www.emergentmind.com/topics/generative-data-refinement-gdr.

[33] The Legal Boundaries of AI Training Data Licensing Contracts. Zhaoxin Contract, May 1, 2025. https://www.zhaoxinms.com/html/web/fawutiandi/1917870616900366338.html.

[34] Protected Material Detection Filter. Microsoft Learn Official Website, November 17, 2025. https://learn.microsoft.com/zh-cn/azure/ai-foundry/openai/concepts/content-filter-protected-material.

(5) Define Copyright Liability Attribution and Clarify Compliance Obligations of Platforms and Users

For example, Baidu's compliance framework for Ernie reflects the approach of an established Chinese internet enterprise. Its Ernie User Agreement and Privacy Policy detail potential compliance risks and highlight user-focused clauses with bold formatting.[35] The agreement clarifies Baidu's ownership of intellectual property rights (software, technology, trademarks) related to its services, while users retain rights to their input content and legally compliant output. It also requires users to refrain from inducing non-compliant output or bypassing platform filters; users bear full legal liability for copyright disputes arising from infringing prompts or unlabeled AI-generated content.

Moonshot, a rising star in large language model development, emphasizes the intellectual property of generated content, input/output data, and user information in its Kimi model's compliance framework. Its Model Service Agreement and User Privacy Agreement concisely define relevant rights and obligations.[36] The agreement stipulates that user data for Kimi's training does not affect the original author's copyright, and Kimi-generated content is limited to non-commercial use (consistent with "fair use" under the Copyright Law). If users violate the agreement by using content commercially, they assume full responsibility for copyright maintenance and any resulting infringement or losses, with Moonshot disclaiming liability. Reporters comparing user agreements of Kimi, Tencent Yuanbao, and other AI products note that "users retain copyright of generated content + assume compliance liability" has become an industry consensus in China. Such clauses aim to standardize user prompt input, reduce infringing content, and protect developers from endless disputes—striking a practical balance between AI development and copyright protection.[37]

(6) Establish a Copyright Compliance Department and Conduct Regular Employee Training

Baidu has long invested in copyright compliance, establishing a Copyright Management Center. This department not only builds the copyright compliance system for generative AI (e.g., Ernie) but also leads the development of an anti-piracy "DNA Comparison and Recognition System," ensuring the copyright compliance of training data and generated content through technology. To meet the copyright needs of its AI-generated short video business, ByteDance established a compliance department with an infringement research team. The team tracks

[35] Ernie User Agreement. Ernie Official Website, March 15, 2025. https://yiyan.baidu.com/infouser#undefined.

[36] Kimi User Service Agreement. Kimi Official Website, October 24, 2025. https://www.kimi.com/user/agreement/modelUse?version=v2.

[37] Tencent Yuanbao Revises User Agreement Three Times: Who Owns Your Chat Records with AI? China Business Journal, March 5, 2025. https://www.toutiao.com/article/7478251624209596967/?upstream_biz=doubao&source=m_redirect.

infringement-related hot topics and risks, clarifies data crawling paths for infringing content, identifies gaps in platform rules and product functions, and optimizes algorithmic and machine review models to improve the accuracy of infringement signal recognition and recall.

(7) Innovate AI Development Technology to Reduce Infringement at the Source

Adopt Innovative Training Methods to Avoid Verbatim Memorization: For example, the "Goldfish Loss" technology used in the Apertus model by the Swiss AI Initiative randomly masks approximately 2% of vocabulary in training text. This prevents mechanical copying of original content while preserving the model's ability to learn language rules and knowledge logic. Experiments show that even after 128 exposures to the same text, the technology effectively avoids verbatim memorization, with model performance matching or slightly exceeding traditional training in multi-language tasks and text generation—ideal for training data containing large amounts of copyrighted text.[38]

Develop Refined Content Fingerprint Engines for Multi-Format Content: For text, software like DeepCompare uses content feature fingerprinting—normalizing documents, extracting semantic features (keywords, paragraph structure), and generating fingerprints via segmented hashing algorithms. It accurately identifies text similarity after modifications (e.g., paragraph rearrangement, format changes) and is widely used in contract review and paper plagiarism checks. For videos, ByteDance's content recognition system for short video copyright generates a unique "content fingerprint" for each uploaded video. The system compares fingerprints with a genuine video library to identify infringing versions (remakes, edits, speed changes), allowing copyright holders to take down infringing content or share advertising revenue—adapting to the mass upload and rapid dissemination of short videos.[39]

Embed Exclusive Watermarks and Fingerprints During Model Development:

White-box watermarking: A technology where model owners verify copyright by accessing internal features (structure, weight parameters) of suspected models, with the core logic of "embedding parameters for extraction and verification." Encrypted signatures are embedded in the model's weight matrix, enabling verification in under 50 milliseconds for rapid ownership confirmation. For example, customized Stable Diffusion models embed watermarks in the LoRA module of the U-Net architecture via the AquaLoRA algorithm before open-sourcing. Images

[38] Swiss AI Initiative Apertus: 15 Trillion Data Rewrites LLM Training Rules. Top AI Lab, October 13, 2025. https://www.toutiao.com/article/7560706014052368911/?upstream_biz=doubao&source=m_redirect.

[39] Technical Systems in the Short Drama Industry Chain—Digital Watermarking and Content Fingerprint Recognition. CSDN, December 19, 2024. https://blog.csdn.net/weixin_41429382/article/details/144209128.

generated using the model carry hidden watermarks, allowing owners to trace the model source and prevent unauthorized commercial use.[40]

Black-box fingerprinting: A technology where model owners verify copyright by inputting specific data and observing outputs (without accessing internal parameters), with the core logic of "implanting trigger associations for output verification." Model fingerprints are formed by calculating input-output hash values; high matching with other models' outputs serves as key evidence for infringement.[41] Huawei Cloud applies this technology in its AI models to protect its intellectual property and prove the independence of generated content in disputes, reducing legal risks.

4.3.2 *Operators*

(1) Pre-Use Material Control and User Notification

AI operators shall assume obligations of material review and rights/liability notification. For material review, operators must implement differentiated audits of user-uploaded materials and published models based on technical feasibility, strengthening authorization verification for high-risk IP materials. For notification, operators must fully inform users of copyright rules for material use and commercial content through clear agreement clauses and step-by-step confirmation processes.

In the aforementioned "Fights Break Sphere Medusa" case, the AI image generation platform explicitly stipulated in its user agreement that users bear copyright liability for uploaded training materials and published LoRA models, defining liability boundaries through pre-notification; it also established a publication review mechanism to conduct compliance screenings of models and generated content on the platform. Overseas, Adobe's Firefly platform controls material compliance from the source: it restricts model training data to authorized content from Adobe Stock and public domain content with expired copyrights, explicitly stating that user personal content is not used for training, and pays remuneration to material contributors—eliminating infringement risks at the data source. Midjourney, an AI painting platform, refines commercial copyright rules: free users must attribute AI-generated content for commercial use, enterprise clients exceeding revenue thresholds need additional authorization, and clear prompt usage guidelines are provided—requiring users to obtain authorization for content involving others' copyrights. By clarifying rules in advance and controlling material sources, such AI operators reduce copyright infringement risks at the source.

(2) Output Content Labeling and Traceability

---

[40] Weitao Feng, Wenbo Zhou, Jiyan He, et al. AquaLoRA: Toward White-box Protection for Customized Stable Diffusion Models via Watermark LoRA. May 2024. https://arxiv.org/list/cs/2024-05?skip=4750 (arXiv:2405.11135 [cs.CR]).

[41] Chenqi et al. [10].

On one hand, AI operators must use technical means to ensure full-process traceability of generated content, including key information such as input prompts, generation parameters, and review records. On the other hand, they must strictly comply with the Measures for the Labeling of AI-Generated Synthetic Content, distinguishing scenarios for explicit and implicit labeling: publicly disseminated content must carry easily identifiable explicit labels to help the public quickly distinguish AI-generated from human-created content; commercial content must additionally embed implicit traceability information to meet copyright verification and liability determination needs.

For example, Adobe Firefly automatically attaches Content Credential digital labels to generated content, clearly indicating the creation method and AI usage to ensure copyright transparency.[42] The AI company involved in the Hangzhou "AI Ultraman" infringement case also added AI-generated content labels in subsequent compliance optimizations, explicitly distinguishing AI-generated from original content and reducing infringement disputes caused by confusion. By achieving content traceability through technical means, such operators not only comply with regulatory requirements for AI-generated content labeling but also provide clear evidence for copyright liability determination.

(3) Infringement Complaint Response and Post-Incident Disposal

AI operators may establish complaint channels, set reasonable disposal time limits based on platform scale and technical capabilities, and immediately take measures such as removing or blocking clearly infringing content. They may also set up compensation funds or purchase copyright insurance to provide infringement protection for users' legal use of generated content, clarifying the scope of protection and liability division to avoid unlimited liability.

For example, upon receiving an infringement lawsuit, a platform operator promptly removed all infringing models, updated review keywords, and notified overseas partner platforms sharing data—ensuring smooth infringement feedback channels and avoiding being found liable for subjective fault due to delayed response. Overseas, GitHub Copilot provides copyright compensation protection: if generated code triggers an infringement lawsuit, the platform assumes liability for rights protection and compensation, establishing a risk safety net for users and itself.[43] By quickly addressing infringement issues and providing liability protection, such operators effectively reduce losses from copyright disputes. However, they must retain complete records of disposal processes as evidence of fulfilling loss mitigation obligations, in line with the "duty to mitigate damages" in fault liability determination.

(4) Strengthen Risk Early Warning and Compliance Review

---

[42] Adobe Inc. Content Credentials Overview. Adobe Help Center, February 17, 2025. https://helpx.adobe.com/uk/firefly/using/content-credentials.html.

[43] Rare Earth Juejin. GitHub Copilot Fully Upgraded with AI Agent Mode, Supporting MCP | Devin 2.0 Released. Rare Earth Juejin, April 9, 2025. https://juejin.cn/post/7491119050136977445.

Combining industry infringement characteristics, AI operators may use technical tools such as AI detection and risk mapping to conduct early warning and interception of high-risk content in input materials and prompts. They should verify material authorization at the input stage, screen for similar content at the generation stage, and control dissemination channels at the publication stage.

For example, AI companies may establish a well-known IP risk prompt mechanism to warn users in advance of high-risk infringing materials, avoiding unintentional infringement. Overseas, GitHub Copilot integrates tools like Snyk Code to detect open-source license issues in generated code, enhancing compliance review of output content. DeviantArt has established a user material authorization review mechanism: for artistic works uploaded by users for AI training, it verifies whether authorization from the original author has been obtained, blocking the inflow of infringing materials at the input stage. By proactively avoiding potential copyright risks through technical screening and risk early warning, such operators improve the full-process compliance control system.

(5) Establish Copyright Authorization Docking Mechanisms and Promote Industry Collaboration and Copyright Information Sharing

AI operators may establish official cooperation with collective management organizations (e.g., Music Copyright Society of China) to build a "one-click authorization" channel. For high-frequency materials such as images, texts, music, and video clips used by users, they may offer flexible authorization plans such as pay-per-use or monthly subscriptions—allowing users to complete authorization purchases on the platform and directly use them for prompt input or model training, eliminating unintentional infringement at the source.

Operators may also co-establish a "high-risk copyright material database" with peer platforms, aggregating core information such as well-known IPs, original works, and paid content to achieve data interconnection. When any platform detects new infringing materials, it can synchronize them to the database for the entire industry to reference and intercept. For copyright holders, operators may establish an "infringement early warning linkage mechanism," inviting publishers, original authors, etc., to settle on the platform and open exclusive copyright monitoring channels. Copyright holders can real-time check whether there is generated content involving their works on the platform, communicate and dispose of it in advance, and avoid disputes caused by the spread of infringing content.

(6) Deepen Internal Compliance and User Guidance Management

Based on actual conditions, AI operators may compile a Platform Copyright Compliance Operation Manual, clarifying differentiated copyright requirements for different user types (individual free users, commercial paid users, enterprise users). For example, individual users are prohibited from commercializing generated content, and enterprise users must retain authorization documents for at least 3 years—with mandatory pop-up prompts for reading during user registration and first commercial use.

Operators may also launch copyright compliance incentive programs: users who strictly abide by copyright rules, proactively complete material authorization, and actively label AI-generated content are rewarded with points, discounts on paid functions, etc. Conversely, users who repeatedly upload infringing materials or evade labeling obligations are subject to tiered penalties such as restricted generation times or account bans—guiding users to form compliant habits.

4.3.3 Users

(1) Strengthen Creation Originality and Retain a Complete Evidence Chain

To obtain copyright protection for AI-generated content and avoid infringement disputes, the core requirement for users is to invest substantial intellectual labor and fix relevant evidence. For example, simply entering a general prompt like "draw a fox" is unlikely to be recognized as original due to the lack of personalized expression.

In September 2025, the Tianshan District People's Court of Urumqi ruled on an AI-generated image copyright dispute, holding that images "one-click generated" by AI software do not constitute works under the Copyright Law. The judgment clarified that under the current copyright system, content fully generated by AI without substantial intellectual input from the creator cannot be protected as a work. In explaining the law, the judge pointed out that if there is evidence that the user has integrated independent ideas, made creative modifications, and other intellectual investments, making the result reflect their unique expression, the relevant generated content may constitute a protected work.[44]

In Jiangsu's first AIGC copyright dispute case (Banxin), the court verified the plaintiff's creation platform login records, prompt modification traces, and other iterative processes during the trial. It determined that the plaintiff's actions such as adjusting prompts and PS retouching reflected their unique creative choices and arrangements, and thus the generated Banxin floor plan had originality and qualified as a work of fine art protected by the Copyright Law.

Therefore, AI users must retain complete creation traces, including prompt documents, parameter setting records, and content iteration versions, and may use blockchain certification tools to solidify these data. Additionally, if the generated content meets originality requirements, users may proactively complete copyright registration to further strengthen their rights and respond to potential ownership disputes.

(2) Strictly Control Copyright Risks in Input and Output Links

[44] Is AI "One-Click Image Generation" Legally Protected? Judge: AI Cannot Replace the Creator's Original Contribution and Is Not Within the Scope of Intellectual Property Protection. Xinjiang Net, November 18, 2025. http://m.toutiao.com/group/7573869114117145142/?upstream_biz=doubao.

At the input stage, AI users must refrain from using unauthorized materials as the basis for AI creation. For example, arbitrarily using popular IP images (e.g., Ultraman) or 截取 classic video clips as generation templates through AI's "image overlay" function may constitute infringement. Users should prioritize materials with no copyright disputes, such as those under the CC0 license (Creative Commons Zero 1.0 Universal—a global copyright waiver protocol where copyright holders voluntarily give up most rights to their works, allowing anyone to use them globally without restriction or remuneration, no prior authorization required, and no attribution necessary). Resources from platforms like Pexels and Pixabay reduce risks at the source. Using CC0 materials for training input or generation reference eliminates the need to verify authorization chains, pay fees, or worry about subsequent liability—resolving the core risk of unclear material copyright.

At the output stage, users must be vigilant against substantial similarity between generated content and others' works. For example, imitating Van Gogh's painting style usually does not constitute infringement, but if the generated content is highly consistent with the original work in composition and core details, it may infringe others' copyrights. Extra caution is required in commercial scenarios: tools like Tencent Zhuque AI and Copyleaks can be used to screen for infringement risks, with manual review for high-risk content involving celebrity portraits or trademarks.[45]

(3) Standardize Copyright Authorization Processes and Fulfill Labeling Obligations

AI users in commercial scenarios must clarify the authorization chain to avoid infringement disputes due to defective authorization. In late 2025, Warner Music Group and Suno jointly issued an English cooperation announcement through PR Newswire, detailing core content such as cooperation objectives, authorized model plans, and profit-sharing mechanisms. After the cooperation, users can legally use Warner's artist resources through payment, and the platform's copyright traceability system provides proof of work compliance—reducing liability risks at the source. The announcement also requires all AI-generated songs to embed tamper-proof labels, indicating artist authorization information and creation proportions to avoid audience misunderstanding of the work's source.[46]

Therefore, users must strictly fulfill the labeling obligation for AI-generated content—both a compliance requirement and a reflection of the principle of good faith. In accordance with China's Measures for the Labeling of AI-Generated Synthetic Content, explicit labeling can be done by adding watermarks to images or labeling the start of videos; metadata such as tool names and timestamps can also be embedded to avoid copyright disputes.

[45] How to Legally Conduct Commercial Creation Using AI Image Generation? Tencent Cloud Developer Community, August 25, 2025. https://cloud.tencent.com/developer/techpedia/2538/19930.

[46] Warner Music Group Corp. Warner Music Group and Suno Forge Groundbreaking Partnership. PR Newswire, November 25, 2025. https://www.prnewswire.com/news/warner-music-group-corp./.

(4) Use Advanced Technical Tools to Reduce Infringement Risks

AI users can leverage technological empowerment to reduce infringement risks throughout the entire process from generation to publication through precise detection and tamper-proof certification. In addition to basic plagiarism checking tools, users can access vector search engines like Milvus. As an open-source cloud-native vector database, Milvus excels in efficiently processing similarity searches of large-scale unstructured data (images, texts, etc.) and is widely used in copyright infringement detection and content traceability. Its distributed architecture supports millisecond-level comparison of tens of millions of vectors.[47]

For example, enterprise users generating e-commerce posters can use such tools to calculate the cosine similarity between generated images and copyright image libraries, setting the threshold below 0.7 to avoid substantial similarity risks (cosine similarity is a common core method for comparing image feature vectors, measuring similarity by calculating the cosine of the angle between two vectors, with values ranging from 0 to 1 (1 = identical). In visual content copyright detection, the threshold is usually set between 0.6 and 0.7 to define "non-substantial similarity"). Self-media practitioners generating copy with AI can use models like Sentence Transformer to generate text embedding vectors, comparing them with published work libraries to screen out highly semantically similar content in advance.

Users may also calculate MD5 hash values for core AI-generated data (e.g., seed values, prompts, sampling steps) and upload them to blockchain platforms like Ant Chain or Tencent Zhixin Chain for certification. Since the certification data of these platforms is connected to judicial blockchain systems, it is often used as key evidence by courts in intellectual property disputes, further confirming the judicial validity of this certification method. For example, a Shanghai SaaS company specializing in AI-generated e-commerce posters received an infringement claim email alleging "highly consistent style." It exported server logs corresponding to the disputed posters, completed blockchain certification through hash calculation, and used the complete evidence chain to prove the independence of its generated content in response to malicious claims.

(5) Comply with Region-Specific Copyright Laws and Special Requirements

Users using generative AI across borders must adapt to differentiated copyright rules in different countries and regions. For example, India plans to implement new regulations in December 2025, requiring payment of copyright fees to collective management organizations for using copyrighted content to train AI. Users commercializing AI-generated content in India must ensure that the training materials relied on have completed paid authorization.[48]

---

[47] Luga Lee. Decoding the Future Foundation of Vector Search: A Comprehensive Understanding of Cloud-Native Database Milvus. Tencent Cloud Developer Community, July 8, 2025. https://cloud.tencent.com.cn/developer/article/2538386.

[48] India Plans to Introduce New Rules: OpenAI, Google and Other Companies Must Pay for Using Copyrighted Content to Train AI. Phoenix Network Technology, December 10, 2025. https://tech.

Breaking away from the current European and American policies centered on "fair use" and "transparency obligations," the new regulations adopt a "mandatory payment + unified management" approach—reducing transaction costs for the AI industry while protecting creators' rights and providing a new solution to the copyright issue of large-scale AI training data. This requires AI users to verify the copyright policies of target regions in advance before cross-border creation or commercial use to avoid compliance risks.

4.3.4 Public Sector

(1) Industry Associations Formulate Compliance Guidelines

The current lack of compliance capabilities among AI enterprises mainly stems from the combined contradictions between legal abstraction and technical black-box characteristics. Unified industry compliance guidelines can provide enterprises with actionable operational standards by clarifying data compliance processes and algorithm transparency requirements.

Domestically, the National Technical Committee for Standardization on Social Application and Evaluation of Intelligent Technologies (SAC/SWG35) takes the lead in formulating the Guidelines for Compliance Management of Service Providers on Social Impacts of Generative Artificial Intelligence Technology Application. Proposed for development in 2024, this guideline is jointly formulated by representatives of leading domestic generative AI enterprises, experts, and scholars, with an expected completion date of 2026. It clarifies specific requirements such as data source verification, copyright risk assessment, and infringement disposal procedures, reducing the risks of AI training data infringement and generated content infringement at the source, and protecting the legitimate rights and interests of copyright holders.

Therefore, judicial rules from typical cases (e.g., the determination standard of "substantial human participation") can be incorporated into the guideline in collaboration with internet courts in cities like Hangzhou and Beijing. For instance, it can explicitly stipulate that prompt iteration records and parameter adjustment trajectories can serve as evidence of originality, ensuring the guideline not only aligns with the spirit of the law but also meets judicial needs.

(2) Establish a Collective Copyright Management Mechanism

In the UK, the Copyright Licensing Agency (CLA), the Authors' Licensing and Collecting Society (ALCS), and the Publishers' Licensing Services (PLS) jointly launched a collective licensing framework for AI training. Adopting an opt-in model, this framework requires right holders to voluntarily join by registering their works; unregistered works are not covered by the license.

---

ifeng.com/c/8oxlvnCFESd.

Previously, the government-proposed opt-out model required creators to actively declare that their works should not be used for AI training, failing which it would be deemed as implied consent. This model faced strong opposition from creators, who argued it imposed an excessive burden on them. In contrast, the new opt-in model not only conforms to protection rules in the field of intellectual property rights but also enables right holders to independently decide whether their works participate in the licensing through a clear voluntary registration mechanism, preventing the disguised encroachment of their rights and interests.[49]

Meanwhile, the framework explicitly designates the CLA to manage the entire licensing process, collecting and distributing royalties to right holders after deducting operational costs. This arrangement is rational: as a recognized collective management organization for textual content in the UK, the CLA has over 40 years of experience in collective licensing, providing long-term authorization services for the creative industry and content users. Its mature royalty collection and distribution mechanism ensures that fees are accurately allocated to authors represented by the ALCS and publishers represented by the PLS, avoiding issues such as royalty retention or unfair distribution.

Therefore, existing institutions can be leveraged to upgrade AI-specific services. For example, we can promote the establishment of an AI Copyright Management Division within existing organizations such as the Music Copyright Society of China and the China Written Works Copyright Society, avoiding redundant construction. We can also adopt the core logic of the UK's opt-in model, where right holders can be included in the distribution system after registering on the AI Work Registration Platform of the National Copyright Administration. Additionally, referring to the Indian model, a designated institution by the National Copyright Administration can formulate unified royalty rates and disclose fund flow to ensure transparency.

(3) Build a Copyright Dispute Mediation Platform

The China Copyright Protection Center and Ant Chain have jointly built the Digital Copyright Chain. Ant Chain's copyright protection product "Quezao" realizes copyright confirmation upon work release through blockchain technology, and can also complete services such as infringement monitoring and electronic evidence collection with AI algorithms. The copyright-related service system developed through their collaboration can verify core data of generated content and handle copyright disputes.

Similarly, to establish and improve a new multi-resolution model for copyright disputes, the Hangzhou Copyright Protection and Industry Development Promotion Association has settled in the Hangzhou Internet Court to carry out the multi-resolution of copyright disputes. It has also set up the Hangzhou Copyright Dispute Multi-Resolution Center. The establishment of this center marks another step forward for Hangzhou in innovating copyright dispute mediation mechanisms and

[49] Kretschmer et al. [11].

improving digital and intelligent governance capabilities, providing a Hangzhou solution for the litigation-mediation mechanism of copyright disputes across the province.

References

1. Heqi W (2025) Path Selection for Copyright Data Protection from the Perspective of Generative Artificial Intelligence. Editorial Friend 6
2. Linghan Z, Lin Y (2025) Division of infringement liability in the value chain of generative artificial intelligence. Journal of Beijing Administration Institute 5
3. Jinliang G (2025) Civil liability for "information errors" in generative artificial intelligence services. Tribune of Political Science and Law 2
4. Hu K, Ludi J (2025) Research on copyright infringement liability of providers of artificial intelligence-generated content services. Journal of Huazhong University of Science and Technology (Social Science Edition) 5
5. Wenyi D, Dongmei X (2025) Copyright law responses to generative AI training data: compliance solutions. Documentation,Information & Knowledge 1
6. Chengjie L (2025) Approaches to attributing AI infringement liability from a typological perspective. Journal of Law Application 3
7. Bingyin F (2025) Is "stealing books" a "Noble crime"?—research on generative AI infringement liability. Digital Law 2
8. Kaizhong H, Ludi J (2024) Copyright disputes and responses to generative artificial intelligence machine learning. Copyright Theory and Practice 9:44–53
9. Jianfeng C (2023) Toward trustworthy AI: governance challenges and responses to ChatGPT-like generative artificial intelligence. Journal of Shanghai University of Political Science and Law (The Rule of Law Forum) (4)
10. Chenqi X, Baowen Z, Ping Y (2021) A survey of artificial intelligence model watermarking research. Computer Science 7
11. Kretschmer M, Meletti B, Bently L et al (2025) Copyright and AI in the UK: opting-in or opting-out? GRUR International 74(10)

Chapter 5
The "Three-Three Matrix" of Artificial Intelligence

Generative artificial intelligence evolves from conception to application through roughly three phases: The first is the collection process, involving access to and replication of existing texts, achieved through acquiring public materials, purchasing corpora, and scraping data to gather foundational materials for AI training. The second phase is the training process, where the aforementioned materials are analyzed and processed to train a big data model that exhibits certain behavioral patterns. The third phase involves responding to user inquiries by generating textual information. These three links are interconnected yet distinct, encompassing various utilizations of "text," "information," and "data" by AI "technology developers," "service providers," and "users." This forms a "Three-Three Matrix," making the copyright infringement issues of generative AI complex and diverse, necessitating a reevaluation of this "Three-Three Matrix" to restore the original usage of works by artificial intelligence.

5.1 The "Three-Three Matrix"

5.1.1 The Tripartite Division of Objects

The distinction among the three objects is the first issue to be addressed within the "Three-Three Matrix." Unlike the certainty of subjects and the patternization of phases, the terms "text," "information," and "data," though commonly encountered in studies of AI copyright infringement, are often used interchangeably without clear differentiation, leading to a lack of targeted research and evidence on whether the objects used by AI coincide with those protected by copyright law.

The relationship among these three objects hinges on "information," referring to the meaning contained within data and messages. For example, the sentence "The

L. Cheng, *Copyright Issues Related to Generative Artificial Intelligence (AI)*, Artificial Intelligence and the Rule of Law,
https://doi.org/10.1007/978-981-95-8781-0_5

Earth is round" contains geographic "information" that the Earth's shape is spherical. At the same time, this sentence is a piece of "text" composed of five characters. Similarly, although the expression "Light exhibits wave-particle duality" can be rephrased as "Both wave and particle properties are fundamental attributes of light," the information or quantity of information does not change. A single piece of information can be expressed in multiple ways, understandable to humans as text. In essence, text is the textual expression of information. If a single piece of text or a collection thereof is original, it is considered a work protected by copyright.

The reason for expressing information as text is that information itself is abstract and can only be concretized and understood through text and characters. Information that is not concretized cannot be understood by humans or recognized by computing programs. Generative AI, based on binary digital algorithms, implies that information must be encoded into numbers to serve as input for computing programs. For instance, GPT-4.0's widespread application is attributable to the construction of the GPT (Generative Pre-training Transformer) model. The essence of generative AI's ability to facilitate human-machine interaction lies in the Transformer within GPT, which converts user inputs such as text and images into a series of numbers using an Encoder. Through computations, ChatGPT generates new numbers and, with the help of a Decoder, converts these numbers back into text, images, etc., to answer user inquiries. If texts like "apple" and "round" are inputted into AI, they cannot be understood or used for training unless they are "digitized" to convert "information" into symbols that the computer can process. AI can further algorithmically explore and quantitatively analyze these "data." If information is considered the essence of data, then data is essentially the digital expression of information. The same piece of "information," when expressed in text, is understood by humans, but when expressed digitally, it is used by artificial intelligence.

Clarifying the relationships among "text," "information," and "data" enables an understanding that the essence of generative AI's use of works is to encode texts carrying specific information into data, which is then used to train artificial intelligence. In copyright law, the abstract ideas carried by original information are protected. However, copyright law does not protect abstract ideas, only their expression. In the digital age, the expression of ideas (information) has branched into two: textual expression forming texts and digital expression forming data. Traditional copyright law protects the former, while whether the latter falls under copyright protection requires analysis of the role of data in the collection, training, and output stages of AI.

5.1.2 The Tripartite Division of Stages

The tripartite division of the object aims to verify that the training of generative artificial intelligence requires a variety of "information" and extensive collection of "text," but the training object is actually "data" rather than "text." How these three elements play a role in the training and use of generative artificial intelligence needs further analysis of the three stages of artificial intelligence operation.

The reason why the output content of generative artificial intelligence is generative, rather than simply copying and pasting, is attributed to the steps of pre-training. In order to ensure that the output content is understandable natural language for humans, ChatGPT's pre-training process mainly includes the following key steps: (1) Data Collection and Processing: Collecting a large amount of text data from various sources such as books, websites, and news. (2) Pre-training Tasks: Using the Transformer architecture for self-supervised learning and training. For example, predicting masked vocabulary in the text, known as the "Masked Language Model" (MLM) practice. (3) Optimization and Adjustment: The model continuously optimizes during pre-training to improve its understanding and generation capabilities of language. (4) Evaluation and Testing: The model is evaluated on multiple standardized test sets to ensure its performance meets expectations. These tests cover various language processing tasks such as text comprehension, translation, and question answering. (5) Fine-tuning: After pre-training, the model is fine-tuned for specific applications. For example, to improve understanding of a specific language or domain, relevant datasets are used for further training. (6) Output generation of text content. These steps 2, 3, 4, and 5 are all aimed at training artificial intelligence to be "smarter" and "more powerful," albeit with different focuses. Therefore, the core steps of artificial intelligence development and use are three: the text collection stage, the data training stage, and the text output stage. In these three stages, there are two basic changes: the transformation of text into data and the transformation of data into text.

In the text collection stage, artificial intelligence requires a large amount of textual resources (usually literary works, but also including databases, dictionaries, thesauri, etc.) to capture the habits of real-world language. At this stage, the text is mainly provided by developers, often using "crawler" technology to crawl massive data on the Internet, including scanning inputs of some physical literature. However, regardless of the method, this stage involves the technical replication of existing texts for information collection, inevitably raising the possibility of copyright infringement. After the artificial intelligence is trained and put into use, users can also upload text to generative artificial intelligence such as ChatGPT for analysis. This process also involves potential infringement of copyright in the original works.

The collection of text information is to train the large language models of generative artificial intelligence. Specifically, the construction of the model during the training stage includes the following five steps: (1) Corpus Compilation; (2) Corpus Preprocessing; (3) Corpus Annotation; (4) Model Training; (5) Formation of a permanent model. During corpus compilation (step 1), appropriate annotations can avoid confusion of various languages collected, categorizing corpora from different languages. During preprocessing (step 2), the corpus preprocesses the collected data to convert text content into a format that can be processed (usually pure text file format). During this stage, images, tables, and other non-text elements are excluded. During annotation (step 3), annotations are made using different categories of tags (grammar, morphology, syntax, etc.) to help the artificial intelligence "understand" correct grammar and usage in specific contexts. During training (step 4), pure text is converted into numbers and data recognizable by algorithms. The annotated corpus is analyzed by algorithms, extracting a set of definitions, probabilities, syntax, and semantic features of word sentences used in specific contexts, which are ultimately stored in the entire model. During model creation (step 5), the trained model is created as a permanent model. The trained model can be regarded as a collection of annotated corpora based on statistical observations. Unlike the "access" and "copying" behaviors in the collection stage, the training stage involves direct use of the corpus, making it the most contentious stage for copyright disputes.

The third stage is the output stage of text content, namely answering user questions. This stage demonstrates the training results based on artificial intelligence training. For example, users can ask ChatGPT to imitate Mo Yan or O. Henry to write a short story, or even answer professional questions in various fields. In the output stage, if the generated content is substantially similar in expression to the original work, it may infringe on the author's copyright. If new expressions are formed while retaining the expression of the original work, there is also a risk of infringement of adaptation rights.

By examining the three stages, it can be understood that there is a possibility of copyright infringement in the "collection," "training," and "output" stages of generative artificial intelligence, and the "collection" of text serves the "training" of artificial intelligence, while the "output" of text is the display of the "training" results, making the training stage the core of generative artificial intelligence. However, the training purposes of generative artificial intelligence are not entirely consistent. For example, the real-time digital simulation system of the National Energy Large Power Grid Technology Research and Development (Experimental) Center is a purely scientific research purpose-trained artificial intelligence system, while HathiTrust in the United States serves the public interest. ChatGPT, on the other hand, is trained for commercial use purposes. In foreign precedents, artificial intelligence training for scientific research purposes is generally not considered copyright infringement, as it encourages scientific innovation, which benefits all humanity or society's public welfare. Therefore, the training of artificial intelligence serving the public has not been recognized as infringement in some precedents. This is also the reason why OpenAI initially chose to register as a non-profit company. In the research and development stage, non-profit and public welfare measures are common methods to avoid compliance and infringement risks. Training artificial intelligence for commercial purposes, however, carries a greater risk of copyright infringement.

5.1.3 The Tripartite Division of Subjects

Research on the object and stages can only address whether artificial intelligence infringes copyright and how it infringes, but further study is needed on the subjects of infringement by artificial intelligence. It should be noted that as of the current development of artificial intelligence, no artificial intelligence possesses what can be called consciousness or thoughts of a subject (human).[1] Therefore, the subject of research is not considered in the study of subjects. The three subjects that may infringe copyright in the development and use of artificial intelligence are: technology developers, service providers, and technology users. All three subjects have an obligation to prevent copyright infringement, but the weight of the obligation and the responsibility vary.

Technology developers, as the research and development team or company of artificial intelligence, are the entities most familiar with whether artificial intelligence uses copyrighted materials and how it uses them. To ensure the intelligence of artificial intelligence, it is necessary to "feed" it with a large amount of high-quality data, such as books, research papers, etc. However, these high-quality data are often protected by copyright law. This puts the technology developers of artificial intelligence in a dilemma. Completely abandoning the input of copyrighted materials would result in limited "intelligence" of the developed artificial intelligence, which does not meet the needs of the industrialization and strategic development of artificial intelligence in various countries. However, disregarding the interests of copyright owners for the sake of the development of artificial intelligence also poses risks of infringing individual rights. During the process of artificial intelligence development, developers often bear the greatest risk of copyright infringement and the obligation of data security.[2] Once the collected text or data is leaked, there is also a possibility of widespread copyright infringement.[3]

Service providers are intermediaries or platforms that connect technology developers and technology users. While safeguarding the rights and interests of technology users, service providers also have an obligation to ensure that the artificial intelligence services they provide do not infringe on the copyrights of others. To this end, it is necessary to prevent copyright infringement risks between service providers and technology developers and between service providers and technology users, with artificial intelligence as the pivot. Forward-looking, when accepting artificial intelligence from technology developers, service providers need to verify as much as possible whether specific artificial intelligence may have a copyright infringement risk, such as requesting technology developers to provide relevant reports and disclose information about copyrighted works used in their research and development process.[4] Backward-looking, when providing artificial intelligence services, service providers need to take necessary management and punishment measures against possible copyright infringement behaviors of users through the signing of service terms, to avoid copyright risks after the deployment of artificial intelligence.

---

[1] See Sun Zhanli: "Analysis of the Legal Personality of Intelligent Robots", published in "Oriental Law" in 2018.

[2] See Wang Ding: "On the Data Security Protection Obligations of Data Processors", published in "Contemporary Law Review" in 2023.

[3] See Jiao Heping: "Copyright Risks and Resolution Paths in Data Acquisition and Utilization in Artificial Intelligence Creation", published in "Contemporary Law Review" in 2022.

[4] In June 2023, the EU "Artificial Intelligence Act (Draft)" added the obligation to disclose copyright information about the use of artificial intelligence in Article 28b.

Compared to technology developers and service providers, technology users have a slightly weaker obligation to avoid copyright infringement, and their likelihood of infringing copyright is also smaller. However, this does not mean that technology users have no risk of infringement. Taking ChatGPT 4.0 as an example, the latest generative artificial intelligence applications can read, learn, rewrite, translate, and summarize text materials uploaded by users. If users upload works of others, there is a risk of copyright infringement. Regarding similar infringement behaviors of users, individual case identification and adjudication can be conducted under existing copyright laws, without much controversy. Therefore, debates about artificial intelligence copyright mainly focus on whether technology developers and service providers should bear responsibility and how to exempt them from liability. To answer questions about the responsibility and obligation division after the "identification" of copyright infringement by generative artificial intelligence, it is necessary to address the solution to "how to determine whether artificial intelligence infringes copyright" as a prerequisite. Therefore, it is necessary to return to the three stages of artificial intelligence for further research, to determine the copyright infringement risks and responsibility-bearing subjects in different stages, in order to derive effective pathways for risk prevention.

5.2 Prohibited Activities During the Collection Phase

In the text collection phase, it is necessary to distinguish between "work access" and "work copying" behaviors. With technological advancements, artificial intelligence can train algorithmic models without copying or storing text, using cloud computing and other methods. Therefore, the risk of infringement during "work access" and "work copying" should be discussed separately.

5.2.1 Avoiding Illegal Access

During text and data mining (TDM), the initial step is accessing the text or data, which can be either freely accessible or restricted. Accessing works is similar to reading books online; mere access without copying or distributing does not typically infringe copyright. However, if a work is protected by "technical protection measures" and even equipped with anti-crawling technologies, then accessing it could violate Article 49 of the Copyright Law as an "intentional circumvention or destruction of technical measures." Moreover, without falling under the exemptions of Article 50 of the Copyright Law regarding the circumvention of technical measures, such illegal access constitutes a copyright infringement. Furthermore, this type of illegal access that breaks through technical protection measures will also be regulated by the "Anti-Unfair Competition Law," "Cybersecurity Law," and "Criminal Law."

In practice, the collection of existing texts by ChatGPT versions before 3.5 was carried out by its founding company, Open AI. The generative AI's need for high-quality text information inevitably involves using existing works, potentially infringing on existing copyrights. Since the advent of GPT 4.0, users can upload texts themselves for the generative AI to analyze, distill core points, and even rewrite parts of existing texts, which undoubtedly increases the potential for copyright infringement. Facing these two different collection behaviors, it's necessary to distinguish between them. Not only the developers of the technology but also the users of generative artificial intelligence must avoid illegal access. In short, illegal access is prohibited by laws of various countries, but it has gained renewed attention during the text collection phase of artificial intelligence.

5.2.2 *Avoidance of Permanent Replication*

Text that is inaccessible cannot be illegally accessed, but the freedom to access text does not necessarily mean that the act of copying or using such content is also free from legal restrictions. In the stage of replication, there is a distinction between temporary and permanent replication. Looking at the latest legislative practices outside of our jurisdiction, Article 4 of the European Union's "Directive on Copyright in the Digital Single Market",[5] for the purpose of TDM, allows for the reproduction and extraction of legally obtained works or other content and retaining them until necessary, i.e., it permits the use of TDM technology for commercial purposes. and Article 35-2 of the South Korean "Copyright Law"[6] have already granted legality to temporary reproduction, that is, collectors may "reproduce, extract, and save legally obtained works and content until necessary". The criterion for distinguishing temporary reproduction from permanent reproduction lies in whether the collected content is always saved in the collector's database and corpus. If the collector deletes the collected texts and data after necessary use, it constitutes temporary copying. Therefore, besides avoiding illegal access, technology developers should also avoid permanent replication of information texts as much as possible.

The reason why many countries tend to preserve a legal space for the text collection of artificial intelligence seems to be choosing the former over the conflict between technological development and existing legal systems, but behind this is more about the maintenance of digital economy development and digital industrial chain. From a global perspective, countries are seeking new points of economic growth. At this moment, science and technology, as the primary productive force, are particularly crucial in the development of artificial intelligence and the drive of

[5] Article 4 of the Directive on Copyright in the Digital Single Market (2016/0280(COD).

[6] South Korean "Copyright Law" Article 35-2: "When a person uses works, etc., on a computer, he or she may temporarily reproduce these works on the computer as necessary for the smooth and efficient processing of information, however, if the use of such works infringes copyright, this provision does not apply."

the digital economy. If copyright owners are given preferential protection in domestic cases, it would force generative artificial intelligence developers to move to other countries to set up bases,[7] leading the country to fall behind others in the new round of technological competition and digital economy race. This is the fundamental reason why various countries are enacting and amending laws to meet the needs of artificial intelligence.

Future copyright or artificial intelligence laws will inevitably need to reserve some space for the development of the industry in terms of the acquisition and use of works, but this does not mean that the collection and use of texts by artificial intelligence will be completely free. Whether to charge a fee and how to charge it still need to be formulated in conjunction with the purpose of the development of artificial intelligence. In this regard, the establishment and operation of Open AI may offer some insights. When Open AI was founded in 2015 as a non-profit company, it did not attract much attention under the banner of scientific research and supporting public welfare, thus avoiding potential copyright litigation disputes. On March 11, 2019, Open AI announced its transformation from a "non-profit" company to a "capped for profit" company and released its first commercial product, the Open AI API, the following year. After entering into commercial operations, disputes over the reproduction and use of works by Open AI have gradually increased.[8]

This indicates that the commercial development of artificial intelligence cannot completely eliminate the risk of copyright infringement due to legitimate access and temporary reproduction. The reason lies in the use of the collected text content, which ultimately yields considerable profits, casting doubt on the necessity for developers to "copy for free" temporarily. The fundamental purpose of accessing and copying text content is to train artificial intelligence, and the nature of the access and copying activities varies depending on the training objectives (scientific research, public welfare, commercial use). Therefore, to mitigate the risk of copyright infringement in artificial intelligence, a comprehensive analysis of its training stage is required.

5.3 The Legitimate Path During the Training Phase

During the training phase, there is a necessary step of converting text into data, which is then used to train artificial intelligence. As such, there exists a path to analyze AI training activities from both the perspectives of existing copyright law and potential future data legislation. Therefore, the discussion is divided as follows.

---

[7] Samuelson [1], p. 158.

[8] See Tremblay, Awad v. OpenAI, Jun. 28, 2023, No. 3:23-cv-03223; Authors Guild, et al. v. OpenAI Inc., Sep. 19, 2023, No. 1:23-cv-08292; The New York Times Company v. Microsoft Corporation, OpenAI, INC., OpenAI LP, OpenAI GP, LLC, OpenAI, llc, OpenAI OPCO LLC, OpenAI Global LLC, OAI Corporation, LLC, and OpenAI Holdings, LLC.

5.3.1 Interpretation of Copyright Law

Existing research often bridges the copyright infringement risks during the AI training phase from angles such as licensing use, statutory licensing, and fair use. However, the issue with licensing use is that the text collection and usage by generative AI are massive and the repeated licensing operations are not only cumbersome but also economically inefficient. Therefore, there are proposals for the collective copyright management of AI, suggesting the establishment of a collective licensing management organization for AI. Unlike collective licensing in the music and film industries, the corpus of AI is huge and covers various fields, making it challenging to establish a collective licensing organization that encompasses all industries or even fields globally. Even if such an organization could be established, its power and structure would be too enormous, turning the management of the organization into a significant challenge. The problem with statutory licensing lies in the scattered nature of the relevant regulations, which primarily include "journal reprinting," "performances by literary and artistic groups," "production of phonograms from sound recordings," and "use of published works by radio stations and TV stations to produce broadcast and TV programs" - categories that are vastly different from the actions of model training and difficult to apply. Moreover, both collective licensing and statutory licensing face the issue of excessively high costs. Even if the fee per transaction is not high, the massive amount of data required by generative AI could lead to prohibitive copyright fees, thereby hampering the research and development of generative AI.[9]

If interpreted from a reasonable use perspective, it also does not conform to the relevant provisions of our country's Copyright Law: First, the twelve scenarios of reasonable use stipulated by the Copyright Law cannot serve as legal grounds to exempt the use of artificial intelligence texts and data. The specific rules involved in the training of generative artificial intelligence models include "personal use," "appropriate citation," "use for study and research," etc. The applicability of the "personal use" rule is strictly limited and cannot be interpreted to cover the commercial development actions of artificial intelligence; the premise for applying the "appropriate citation" rule is "to introduce, comment on, or explain a certain work" or "to illustrate a certain issue," focusing on the characteristics of actions at the output stage, which cannot match the usage characteristics during the training stage of generative artificial intelligence; "scientific research" limits the use of works to "school classroom teaching or scientific research" and also emphasizes that only "a small amount of copying" is permitted, obviously, the behavior of massively copying and using works for data models cannot meet this requirement. Second, although Article 24, Paragraph 1, Item 13 of the Copyright Law stipulates a catch-all clause for reasonable use, the "other circumstances" mentioned in this clause are preceded by "provided by laws, administrative regulations," which is a closed provision.

[9] See Li Qiyuan: "ChatGPT Model Training: Copyright Infringement Dilemmas and Solutions," published in Shanxi Science & Technology News on August 24, 2023, Edition B07.

Judicial interpreters cannot use this clause to interpret and create other scenarios of reasonable use not specified by other laws and administrative regulations. Before the introduction of specialized artificial intelligence legal regulations, this catch-all clause is also difficult to apply.

The classification between "expressive use" and "non-expressive use" is meaningful for reference, but there is room for further explanation regarding the "non-expressive use" of generative artificial intelligence. As mentioned before, both text and data are expressions of information. Between the stages of "collection" and "training," there is a process where text is converted into data. Under the premise of legally collecting text and making temporary copies, the use by artificial intelligence is no longer a textual expression of thoughts and information, but its digital expression. This raises questions about the protection of copyright on expressions of thought: whether copyright only protects the textual expression of thoughts or all expressions of thought. From the perspective of ways to express thoughts, text has never been the only form of expression. Artistic expressions in songs and dances, as well as the coding expression of computer software, are also protected by copyright. Among these, the most similar to machine learning is the study of computer software content. Article 17 of the "Computer Software Protection Regulations" states: "For the purpose of studying and researching the design ideas and principles contained in the software, the use of software through installation, display, transmission, or storage, etc., without the permission of the copyright owner of the software and without paying compensation, does not constitute an infringement of copyright."

Similarly, the act of artificial intelligence using works for training essentially involves converting text into data, then classifying and analyzing the data, and forming a generative large language model with originality. The actions of classification and analysis during the training process aim to determine the probabilities of arrangements and combinations of text or graphics, thus achieving accuracy and anthropomorphism in probabilistic output of text. The large language model thus formed is not a simple copy of existing models or data but the result of data training and learning, similar to the learning of software design ideas and principles. ChatGPT does not understand Tang and Song dynasty poetry; it learns not the creative expression of "a stream that plunges down three thousand feet," but the probabilistic possibilities of the arrangement of these seven characters. Therefore, strictly speaking, the training of generative artificial intelligence is also a form of non-expressive use, and it is a mathematical sense of non-expressive use, not constituting an infringement of copyright.

Japan's latest revision to Article 30-4 of the Copyright Law[10] clearly establishes a system for the fair use of "data training," indicating that data analysis of copyrighted content can constitute fair use, with the precondition that it is "within the

[10] Article 30-4 of the Japanese Copyright Law: "In the following and other cases, where the use of works is not for the purpose of enjoying the thoughts or emotions expressed by the works for oneself or others, the works can be used in any manner within the necessary scope. However, this provision does not apply if, depending on the type and use of the work, the manner of use of the work would improperly harm the interests of the copyright owner."

necessary limits and does not unreasonably harm the legitimate rights and interests of the copyright owner." The judgment of "unreasonable harm" requires the application of the principle of proportionality.[11] Although the provisions of the Japanese Copyright Law consider that the training stage of artificial intelligence involves the analysis and use of data rather than text, they do not completely break away from the interpretation mindset of the existing copyright law's fair use model. This is because if the training stage of artificial intelligence is fully recognized as not infringing copyright, it seems that there might be loopholes in the protection for the rights owners of works.

The legislative purpose of copyright law is not to prohibit all uses of works but to protect and reward copyright owners through a system of free use, paid use, and prohibited use, thereby encouraging creative expression. If the collection, training, and output stages are viewed as a whole, the act of collecting works before training and the imitative text and graphic outputs after training both indicate that the works of copyright owners are being utilized by artificial intelligence. If artificial intelligence's training behavior is deemed to be absolutely fair use or absolutely not infringing copyright, it means that artificial intelligence has obtained a "pass" for free use of all works in the future, which obviously does not align with the individual interests of copyright owners and the overall value pursuit of society. Therefore, the core issue in the artificial intelligence training process is not "whether there is infringement" but "whether there is a charge" and "how to charge." The issue of charging during the artificial intelligence training stage faces the problems of high costs, low efficiency of individual charges, and difficulties in managing unified charges in copyright law. If returning to the essence of the object of artificial intelligence training, it becomes clear that the real subject of charging during the training stage is not "work text" but "massive data," hence a solution might be found from the perspective of data legislation and data charging.

5.3.2 *The Necessity for Data Legislation*

Copyright is not the only right that needs to be protected during the process of artificial intelligence training. Since it involves the use of data, there naturally exists a risk of infringement on data rights by artificial intelligence. Currently, countries are still exploring the ownership of data and its legal protection. In China, the Central Committee of the Communist Party and the State Council's "Opinions on Building a Data Fundamental System to Better Play the Role of Data Elements" (hereafter referred to as "Data Twenty Articles") first proposed the "three rights separation" system of data resource ownership, data processing use right, and data product operation right. Traditionally, entities like The New York Times and literary authors

---

[11] See Zhang Chengu: "Interpretation of the 'Three-Step Test' and 'Fair Use'", Global Law Review, May 2016.

have copyright over their works. However, in the context where artificial intelligence does not directly use the works but the data transformed from the works, traditional copyright owners are also the subjects of data resource ownership. Therefore, it is more appropriate to regulate the training behavior of artificial intelligence from a data perspective. Charging for data and databases can facilitate the sale of data in packages. As the data element market continues to improve,[12] such a data charging method not only better meets the massive data needs of artificial intelligence but also enables data transactions at a cost significantly lower than copyright licensing fees. This allows AI developers to obtain the data processing use right and, to some extent, rewards the intellectual contributions of copyright owners, thus resolving the conflict between the industrial development of artificial intelligence and the protection of individual rights.

When establishing specific charging standards, the dilemma of copyright on this issue must be considered. For generative AI like ChatGPT, if copyright owners impose high licensing fees based on their own will, it will inevitably lead AI developers to use texts that are easy to obtain and have lower acquisition costs. These relatively accessible online resources often lack comprehensiveness or contain biases. For instance, if representative works of a certain culture or group are subject to high copyright fees, AI systems may not be able to fully learn and understand the characteristics of these groups, potentially leading to biased content generation.[13] Therefore, the data use charges for artificial intelligence should avoid self-determination in various fields. With thorough market research, the laws of market operation should be emphasized,[14] to then determine specific charge amounts suitable for the development of the AI industry. Additionally, these charging standards should consider the training and use purposes of artificial intelligence. To encourage the flow and sharing of data,[15] certain degrees of free use permission can be granted for scientific research and public welfare AI data use.

Besides setting charging standards, how to establish a charging management organization is another challenge in addressing the legality of artificial intelligence (AI) training from a copyright perspective. It's not necessary to form a global or industry-wide unified data charging organization for data transactions. Instead, data trading centers can be established to marketize data transactions. Currently, over 30 data exchanges have been constructed nationwide,[16] indicating that future data trading channels will be relatively smooth. However, data trading will not be an

[12] See Chen Jidong: "The Theoretical System and Core Issues of Artificial Intelligence Law," Oriental Law, January 2023 issue.

[13] Levendowski [2], p. 579.

[14] See Huang Shaokun: "The Legitimacy Control of Platform Rules," Journal of Beijing Institute of Technology (Social Sciences Edition), May 2023 issue.

[15] See Ding Xiaodong: "Who Does the Data Really Belong To? — From the Perspective of Web Crawlers, Platform Data Ownership, and Data Protection," ECUPL Journal, May 2019 issue.

[16] Tencent News: "Jointly Building a Unified National Data Element Market: 30+ Data Exchanges Propose," accessed January 14, 2024, https://new.qq.com/rain/a/20231119A0640500.

aggregation of individual transactions, but rather bulk purchases of databases or data collections from data service providers. Apart from free data available online, a vast amount of high-quality data is concentrated in local publishers, journals, and universities. These entities have relatively weak profit motives, making it unlikely for them to become data service providers in the short term. At this juncture, collective organizations need to play a certain promotional role, forming data merchants centered around publishers, journals, universities, etc., and directly connecting with large model companies that have relevant data needs. As the market gradually matures, data service providers will enjoy control and dispossession rights over data due to their labor or other contributions,[17] and participate in market pricing. During the market establishment process, there will inevitably be "market competition" and "market disorder,"[18] suggesting that resolving AI training material disputes from a data perspective requires the collaboration of high-quality data service providers and standardized data exchanges, along with a tolerant and cautious attitude towards innovating AI data commercial charging models.

The data law application pathway for AI training materials could also address a problem left over from the AI collection stage. The objects of AI collection are not only "texts" but also "data" obtained through crawling.[19] Therefore, the rules of legitimate access and temporary copying during the collection phase will also apply to data crawling. Any illegal data crawling behavior and uncharged permanent copying acts are infringements on the rights of data rights holders. In short, data crawling should also be subject to the boundaries of legitimacy.[20]

Although the training of AI involves "non-expressive use" of data, it is undeniable that the mathematical calculations of AI sometimes produce original expressions. How to protect such original expressions is a core issue in the text output stage.

5.4 Copyright Protection in the Output Phase

In the text output stage, copyright interest maintenance is divided into two aspects: firstly, how to avoid AI-generated content infringing on others' copyrights; secondly, how to reasonably allocate the copyright ownership of AI-generated content.

---

[17] See Zhang Suhua, Wang Nian: "The Certification and Construction of a 'Dual-Level Binary Structure' of Data Property Rights," China Law Review, June 2023 issue.

[18] See Xiong Qi, Zhu Ruohan: "The Coordination of 'Autonomy' and 'Regulation' in Internet Copyright Governance," Study and Practice, September 2023 issue.

[19] See Zhang Huibin, Xiao Qixian: "Copyright Exemption Rules Construction for Text and Data Mining in the Age of Artificial Intelligence," Science Technology and Law Chinese-English Version, June 2021 issue.

[20] See Xu Ke: "The Legitimacy and Boundaries of Data Crawling," China Legal Science, February 2021 issue.

5.4.1 *Infringement Risks of Generated Content*

It's undeniable that generative AI possesses a strong "content creation" capability, as outlined by Van Dis et al. in "ChatCPT: Five Priorities for Research" in Nature (2023). Its "output" behavior can be categorized into expressive and non-expressive outputs. The specific distinction depends on whether the AI's generated content merely utilizes the ideas, concepts, and styles contained within the training texts, or it utilizes the expressions of the works. To avoid potential copyright disputes, generative AI does not directly replicate the original texts of others' works but can mimic others' writing styles, resulting in non-expressive use. For instance, ChatGPT would not directly provide the original text of copyrighted works because developers have added necessary protective algorithms to the model post-training to prevent copyright disputes due to high similarity between output and input. This type of learning and outputting in others' styles as non-expressive output is not recognized as infringement under traditional copyright law, thus, AI's non-expressive output should not be considered as infringement.

Another question regarding whether AI-generated content infringes on copyright lies in whether the imitation of a copyright owner's style constitutes substantial similarity to the original works. Substantial similarity does not require the defendant's work to be identical or completely similar to the plaintiff's work. Judges, when determining substantial similarity, often consider from the outcome if the audience of the work can perceive the AI-generated content as originating from a specific work. Once it constitutes substantial similarity, even if the AI's collection and training phases do not constitute copyright infringement, its developers and providers must still bear some copyright infringement liability. This requires future AI technology development to not only avoid direct copying and pasting by AI but also to avoid substantial similarity with prior works as much as possible.

5.4.2 *Ownership of Generated Content*

The "I" in AI and IP stands for Intelligence and Intellectual, respectively. Though differing in grammatical form, both terms denote intelligence and talent. As for Artificial Intelligence (AI), the content it produces may indeed qualify as "Intellectual Property" (IP). Taking ChatGPT as an example, whether the text it "outputs" possesses "originality" and thus falls under intellectual property protection, and to whom this intellectual property belongs, is worth exploring. Strictly speaking, the content generated by generative AI can be divided into works generated under human guidance and those autonomously generated by AI, and the copyright ownership of these two categories needs to be examined separately.

Determining the ownership of works created by AI implies two levels of inquiry: firstly, whether the creations of AI constitute works, and secondly, if they do, to whom do these works belong? Answering the first question necessitates grounding in the definition of "creation." If creativity is not defined as a typical human capability but rather as a set of features or behaviors, then creativity may indeed exist within the code of machines.[21] Currently, AI's creation does not stem from human-like "inspiration" but rather from the model's output of "answers" after precise digital computation. In cognitive science, creativity is often defined as "novelty and usefulness",[22] and creativity is generally considered related to intelligence. However, it is undeniable that some output content of generative AI does possess innovative and practical value and deserves certain protection.

When generating text content under human guidance, AI behaves more like a tool or auxiliary device, with its creative process under direct control and guidance of human creators. For example, if an artist uses an AI program to assist in painting but retains direct control over the style, theme, and final presentation of the work, then the work can be considered as generated under human guidance. In this scenario, the copyright of the work should belong to the human creator because they play a decisive role in the creation process. The role of AI is similar to other creative tools (such as brushes or computer software), with no dispute over copyright ownership.

In cases where AI autonomously generates text content, AI itself makes creative decisions with little or no human intervention. For instance, if an AI program autonomously composes music or writes, and the role of the human creator is limited to initiating the program and setting some basic parameters, then the work can be considered as autonomously generated by AI. The distinction between content generated autonomously and under guidance lies in the extent of human involvement and control in the creative process. In the context of copyright law, this distinction is crucial as it relates to the ownership of works and the definition of creators.

Acknowledging the possibility of AI's independent creativity, research on AI-generated content often discusses whether non-human entities such as AI can be interpreted as "authors" from the perspective of "authorship",[23] and some even propose redefining authors in copyright law.[24] However, when allowing AI to autonomously create works, the relationship between humans and AI is more akin to that of "employer" and "employee" rather than "author" and "co-author." Therefore, the owner of AI[25] should be regarded as the "employer" of AI works, while AI itself should be treated as a type of "employee." In US copyright law, "works made for hire" are those created by employees within the scope of their employment, and the copyright belongs to the employer. Even if AI is not a human employee in the traditional sense, the works it creates should be considered "works made for hire,"

[21] Bridy [3], pp. 395–401. (hereinafter referred to as [3]).

[22] Cave [4], pp. 177–191.

[23] See Wang Qian: "Reconsideration of the Qualification of AI-generated Content in Copyright Law", Tribune of Political Science and Law, 2023, Issue 4.

[24] Fraser [5], pp. 305–333.

[25] AI owner refers to individuals or entities with the right to use AI systems. They may not be directly involved in the programming of AI but own and use it.

thereby attributing the copyright to the owner of AI.[26] In some cases, the owner of AI may be the AI programmer. When AI programmers are directly involved in the design and development of AI systems, they may have strong claims to the copyright of works generated by AI. In such cases, AI programmers may also be considered the rightful copyright owners of the works.[27]

In China, concepts similar to "works made for hire" appear in "duty works" and "commissioned works." However, "duty works" exist between "entities" and "employees," and identifying individuals using ChatGPT as entities is obviously inappropriate. Therefore, from the perspective of commissioned works, if a work is created under a commission relationship, the ownership of copyright is determined by the agreement between the parties to the commission, necessitating that providers of AI services explicitly specify ownership rights of AI-generated works in service agreements. If the agreement does not specify, the copyright typically belongs to the commissioning party. However, ChatGPT is currently difficult to be considered "human", it remains just a creative tool with "ability" but no "intelligence",[28] hence the copyright of autonomously generated content by AI should not be interpreted from the perspective of "commissioned works", "duty works," or "works made for hire". Advanced AI like ChatGPT has not achieved the emergence of true intelligence and belongs to typical advanced computational and analytical tools. Therefore, the works should be attributed to the users or owners of AI.

Another approach is to categorize works independently created by AI as a new category of public property. This means that the law should establish a clear and orderly public domain for works created by AI, classifying AI creations that surpass autonomy thresholds as "machine-generated public property." Such works would not be subject to traditional copyright protection but would become a new type of public resource, helping to distinguish these works from those traditionally created by humans.

References

1. Samuelson P (2023) Generative AI Meets Copyright; Ongoing Lawsuits Could Affect Everyone Who Uses Generative AI. Science 158:19
2. Levendowski A (2018) How Copyright Law Can Fix Artificial Intelligence's Implicit Bias Problem. Wash Law Rev 93:579
3. Bridy A (2016) The evolution of authorship: work made by code. The Columbia Journal of Law & the Arts 39(3):395–401

[26] See Li Weimin: "Reconstruction of the Duty Work System and the Choice of Copyright Attribution Path for AI Works", Law Review, 2020, Issue 3.

[27] Hristov [6], p. 431.

[28] See Cheng Le: "Public and Private Governance of ChatGPT Algorithmic Decision-making", Jingchu Law Review, 2023, Issue 3.

4. Cave R (1970) A combined factor analysis of creativity and intelligence. Multivar Behav Res 5(2):177–191
5. Fraser E (2016) Computers as Inventors: Legal and Policy Implications of Artificial Intelligence on Patent Law. SCRIPTed 13:305–333
6. Hristov K (2016) Artificial intelligence and the copyright dilemma. Idea 57:431

The manufacturer's authorised representative in the EU is Springer Nature Customer Service Centre GmbH, Europaplatz 3, 69115 Heidelberg, Germany. If you have any concerns regarding our products, please contact ProductSafety@springernature.com

Printed and bound by CPI Group (UK) Ltd, Croydon, CR0 4YY
21/09/2026
02219975-0004